# Staff Development Guide

Orlando   Boston   Dallas   Chicago   San Diego

Visit *The Learning Site!*
www.harcourtschool.com

Printed in the United States of America

ISBN 0-15-312768-6

1 2 3 4 5 6 7 8 9 10    082    2003 2002    2001 2000

# CONTENTS

## Vocabulary and Spelling

## Assessment

## School-Home Connection

## Professional Resources

# CREATING AN
# EXEMPLARY CLASSROOM FOR LITERACY GROWTH

BY PATRICIA SMITH

ELEMENTARY READING/LANGUAGE ARTS COORDINATOR, CYPRESS-FAIRBANKS SCHOOL DISTRICT, HOUSTON, TEXAS
AND ADJUNCT PROFESSOR OF EDUCATION, UNIVERSITY OF HOUSTON, CLEAR LAKE CITY

Exemplary classrooms are the result of teachers who make effective decisions about the
- physical classroom arrangement, • social climate, • organization for instruction,
- delivery of information, and • assessment of learning.

## PHYSICAL CLASSROOM ARRANGEMENT

There is certainly no one way to arrange the classroom, but here are some features that can facilitate growth in literacy:

| Feature | Rationale |
| --- | --- |
| Desks arranged in foursomes, or tables | Promotes communication and group work |
| Print-rich environment | Emphasizes the importance of print; provides practice |
| Comfortable, relatively quiet reading area | Encourages sustained silent reading |
| Bookshelves/display areas | Provides access to literature |
| Author's Chair | Promotes writing and sharing; acknowledges authorship |
| Students' products on display | Highlights student work |
| Mailboxes | Promotes student-to-student communication |
| Question and suggestion boxes | Encourages student input; nurtures responsibility |
| Computers | Incorporates technology; promotes editing |
| Learning centers | Promotes inquiry and initiation |

Common in exemplary classrooms is a social climate in which the students feel

- disciplined
- safe in taking risks,
- appreciated,
- needed, and
- motivated.

**Disciplined**   Edmonds (1982) found in his research on effective schools that a climate that is orderly without being rigid is conducive to effective instruction. The orderly climate is upbeat and marked by procedures and rules that are established collaboratively early in the year. Students know what is expected of them because they are involved in setting expectations. Reminder charts are visible. When necessary, the teacher reinforces expectations through procedures such as proximity, eye contact, contracts, positive reinforcement, and parent/guardian contact. The goal is self-discipline.

Is all this time spent trying to establish routines really that important? Wang, Haertel, and Walberg (1994) found that classroom management had more impact on helping students learn than any other variable: "Children who engage in constructive behaviors are more likely to perform well."

**Safe**   There is a sense of security that pervades a well-managed classroom. That feeling of safety is extended when the teacher and students outlaw put-downs and promote risk-taking. Arthur Costa (1984) encourages teachers to convey the unacceptability of "I can't!" or "I don't know how to . . ."

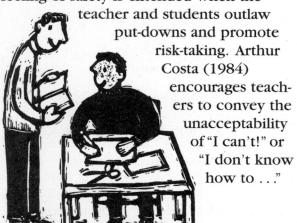

Rather, Costa would have teachers help students identify the information, materials, and skills they need to perform the desired behavior. This helps students persevere and move toward growth.

**Appreciated**   The climate in an exemplary classroom is positive and filled with appreciation. Both teachers and students look for opportunities to use effective praise with one another. Verbal and written feedback, as well as displays of work, celebrations of effort, and time spent listening to one another show this appreciation. Costa (1984) advocates the exemplary practice of helping students evaluate and take credit for work that is well done. He encourages teachers to ask their students, "What have you done that you're proud of?" and "How would you like to be recognized for your achievement?" Students might well choose to have their name on the board, applause, or a note home.

**Needed**   The social, interactive climate of exemplary classrooms emphasizes the importance of each member of the class. All the students have responsibilities and are part of the community of learners. One parent reported that her son begged for an evening dentist appointment so he could be at school and continue his role within his research group.

**Motivated**   The amount of motivation students exhibit is proportional to their perceptions of the usefulness of the experience and of the possibility of success. These two dimensions of motivation are made more likely when there is the opportunity for choice. Teachers in exemplary classrooms look for ways student choice can be exercised in determining the activities undertaken, the resources used, the group members involved, and the format of final presentations.

# ORGANIZATION FOR INSTRUCTION

An exemplary classroom is organized through the integration of the language arts and the use of thematic units, when appropriate, for connecting learning across the curriculum. Most importantly, perhaps, an exemplary classroom is organized to provide all important components of reading and language arts instruction. In such a classroom, plenty of time is scheduled for activities like those in the following chart:

| For Students | With Students | By Students |
|---|---|---|
| Reading Aloud to Students | Strategic or Guided Reading | Sustained Silent Reading |
| | Shared Reading | Other Independent Reading |
| Teacher Modeling | Interactive Strategy Lessons | Student Modeling |
| | Language Experience | Reader Response Activities |
| | Writer's Workshop | Journal Writing |
| | Spelling Lessons and Word Sorts | Spelling Logs |

Note that Linda Fielding and P. David Pearson (1994) recommend that "of the time set aside for reading instruction, students should have more time to read than the combined total allocated for *learning* about reading or *talking or writing* about what has been read." Gary and Maryann Manning (1984) found that recreational reading was most beneficial when the books were

- chosen by students,
- at a slightly challenging level,
- available for rereading, and
- discussed with the teacher and/or peers.

Student groupings for the various components of instruction include whole class, small homogeneous and heterogeneous groups, independent work, and teacher-student or student-student conferences. Flexible grouping allows the benefits of each type of organization to be realized.

# DELIVERY OF INFORMATION

Instruction begins with high academic expectations. In one exemplary classroom, a new student entered who was obviously used to engaging in off-task behavior. "Hey," admonished his classmates, "we don't have time for that stuff; we've got to lot to learn!" How wonderful that the teacher had enrolled the class in the shared vision of academic growth. Needless to say, the new youngster was quickly acclimated and involved in effective instruction and learning.

Effective instruction and learning is

- targeted at priority objectives worth learning,
- delivered at an appropriately challenging level,
- paced to promote success and challenge,
- planned to promote engagement of the learner,
- designed to enable the student to become independent.

A teacher in an exemplary classroom becomes a master at explaining, modeling, questioning, and praising. The instruction moves from teacher modeling through guided practice to independent application. Multi-modality materials such as audio-cassettes, manipulatives, and reminder charts help to address all students' needs.

Cooperative learning also helps students become more successful. The students in cooperative groups work to achieve learning by everyone in their group. They evaluate the learning and the process for the learning.

A variation of cooperative group work was evident in one exemplary class where the fifth-graders were paired with first-grade learning buddies. The fifth-graders were helping the first-graders read about penguins and polar bears. Each pair had a globe, paper cutouts of the animals, and temporary adhesive so they could place the animals on the appropriate locations on the globe. The learning was intense!

Students in exemplary classrooms also engage in inquiry learning, in which they research information that they have a need to know. Investigations and the sharing of information from those investigations are very important to the overall goal of promoting lifelong learning. Motivation from these types of experiences is almost guaranteed! In an exemplary classroom, the learning is never complete. The last question the teacher asks is "What else would you like to know about this topic?"

Student-motivated learning is also promoted when teachers concentrate on developing thinking skills. Students enjoy the problem-solving processes of determining a goal, generating ideas, planning a course of action, taking that action, monitoring progress, and engaging in replanning if necessary. When students choose the goal, thinking and planning become highly purposeful.

When teachers probe for explanations of how the students accomplished a particular answer or task, they are promoting further use of effective thinking. The answer is not nearly as important as the process. In one classroom, the teacher awarded stickers with the message "I know and I know how I know!" when a particularly fine job of explaining the thinking had taken place.

## ASSESSMENT OF LEARNING

In an exemplary classroom, teachers understand that teaching does not automatically result in learning. Since learning is the goal, assessment of the learning must occur to know what needs to be done next. Sometimes students will be ready to take on new topics and strategies; at other times, reteaching with alternative techniques is needed.

Observing student performance helps to make assessment and instruction flow seamlessly. Instruction flows into assessment, which flows into additional instruction. The collection of data in student portfolios allows the teacher, the students, and the students' families to reflect on the learning that is taking place. A key element of portfolio review is student self-evaluation of learning, which seems to increase students' sense of responsibility and ownership. After all, if students are to become lifelong learners, they will need to be lifelong self-evaluators as well.

# HOW TO CREATE Flexible GROUPING

BY DR. LORRAINE GERHART

**"So how do we get the heartbeat of the hallway into the classroom and maximize its potential for language learning?"**

There is little evidence to suggest that grouping or tracking has been successful in creating more literate students. Ability grouping does not address the student as a confident learner and user of language, and teachers want the answers to questions about how to create flexible grouping that will maximize literacy.

### Why are classroom relationships important for flexible grouping?

Time that is taken to build student relationships that are collaborative in nature and show trust will provide a base for effective instructional grouping. Students need guidelines and consistency to balance their growing independence and creativity. Teachers will want to encourage self-monitoring and share control of the classroom to meet the large variety of student needs. Flexible grouping is natural in this situation.

### What activities are most successful in each of the grouping patterns?

**WHOLE GROUP** The whole class can be involved when it is important to develop process outcomes. An effective technique involves using an overhead projector to build a semantic map for the process, asking students to add their contributions and handing out undeveloped maps to the class for their own notes. Guided practice is a must. Presenting minilessons, developing a concept, and providing a model also are effective with the whole group.

Sometimes it works well to divide the whole group into two parts, assigning a role to each part. One half of the room supports an idea while the other half of the room refutes it. Students can present examples and facts from the reading and their opinions to support their viewpoints. If the teacher is developing a concept, it can be effective to assign a particular point of view to each half of the room. For example, one side might present the parent point of view while the other side presents the teenager point of view.

### Whole Group
- Work on process outcomes
- Present minilessons
- Present new knowledge
- Develop a concept
- Share an experience
- Provide modeling
- View a film or video

## Small Group

- Practice processes
- Develop a skill
- Share information
- Elaborate on a concept
- Collaborate on a project
- Discuss and reflect
- Combine research
- Build collaboration skills

## Partners or Pairs

- Reteach a skill or concept
- Reinforce ideas
- Vary pace
- Increase participation
- Interact socially

## Individual

- Exercise self-selection
- Advance at own pace
- Practice a skill independently
- Follow personal interest

## Advantages

- Varying ability levels contribute to the task
- Above and below level readers and writers work together
- A positive learning environment
- Positive peer social interaction

**SMALL GROUP**   The reasons for teaching with small groups are many. This grouping pattern is effective for sharing reading or writing, skill practice, discussion, collaboration, response and reflection, and finding solutions. Small groups are a vehicle allowing students to interact socially and to help one another.

The types of small groups number as many as the variety of activities that are appropriate for that grouping pattern. Depending on your choice of activities, the types of groups assigned might include: enrichment groups, study groups, interest groups, project groups, problem-solving groups, drama or role-playing groups, and even learning-style groups (verbal, artistic, musical . . .).

**PARTNERS or PAIRS**   Pairing students with learning partners for a two- or three-week period can be very helpful. Learning partners can be seated next to each other and can sometimes team up with another set of partners to make a small group. Learning partners teach each other, respond to each other's work, work together, help each other with goals, give support, reinforce ideas, and serve as tutors. Partners provide another way to differentiate instruction.

**INDIVIDUAL**   Although grouping students is very beneficial, there are times when working independently is necessary or preferable. Student-centered curriculum encourages the teaching of topics that are of interest to students. Independent study allows students to choose their own topics to learn about and provides for the most accurate pacing—the student's own pace. Independent practice and application of skills and strategies are also beneficial to those students who need more work in a specific area.

### What are the advantages to varying the grouping pattern?

As you can see, flexible grouping is an effective means to achieve the various outcomes and goals we strive for as teachers. The overall advantages are that cooperative learning allows for all students to participate and contribute, provides for learning and interaction, and is a welcome change of pace.

© Harcourt

## What are some methods to use to form groups or pairs?

Groups are formed at random or by teacher assignment, free choice, similar interest, or special directions. For example, a teacher may direct students to make up a group of two girls and a boy, or two boys and a girl. Allow time for social exploration so that students get to know one another, have opportunities to talk with each other, and develop class unity and respect. Helping students learn how to work with others and setting standards for behavior in the classroom are worth a teacher's time. Asking students to help set the parameters can also be effective.

## What can I do to include the student who inevitably is left out of a group?

Every class is bound to have a difficult student who seems not to fit in with the various groups. Discussing the importance of including everyone in the class may not be sufficient. Sometimes the teacher must intervene by assigning specific groups, asking particular students to work with this person, or having that student work with a resource teacher. Other strategies that might help to include the difficult student are to rotate group members regularly or to fill in absences and to assign that student a specific task which assists all the groups.

## What are some special techniques to ensure fluid and effective grouping within the class?

Flexibility and fluid movement occur when opportunities are provided for varied working patterns. For example, a student can be appointed as a *quiz master* to check a simple assignment, to give a spelling test on a personal word list, to quiz or drill other students on specific knowledge, or to check for understanding. A *row captain* or *group captain* can administer a quick quiz, give an oral quiz, check for understanding, or take responsibility for task completion. Students take pride in helping one another and begin to understand that the work of the classroom belongs to everyone. *Group and regroup* long-term partners and groups or organize subgroups for the day. Appoint or assign individuals or pairs to short-term specific tasks. Include stations or experience posts in the classroom where students can work when they have additional time.

© Harcourt

### Grouping Methods
- Birthdays in the same month
- Same kinds of pet
- Common interests, like a specific sport, a musical group, cars, or bikes
- Drawing numbers
- Working on a specific subject or skill that requires practice

### Including the Difficult Student
- Suggest working with a classmate they have never worked with before
- Teacher-assigned groups
- Ask someone to invite this person
- Assign this student some individual job
- Rotate members
- Trade partners
- Draw numbers

### Special Techniques
- Appoint a quizmaster
- Appoint row or group captains
- Group and regroup as needed
- Use interrupters or signalers

*Interrupters* or *signalers* are needed in a classroom that uses flexible grouping. Flicking the lights, using a bell, tapping on metal, or even making a hand signal can be effective as an interrupter. For example, using the word *FREEZE*, as in the old game of statue-maker, can create a silent classroom. During that freeze, the teacher has 30 seconds to give a terse direction, or students have 30 seconds to return to their original seats after the teacher says "thirty second return." It may take some practice, but students will find the idea of beating the clock a bit of fun that makes the day interesting.

**TIP**  Think through which of your activities you might try in each group format. There is no one right type of group for each instructional goal, but the checklist on the next page gives some examples.

## Matching Activities to Grouping Options

|  | Whole Class | Teacher-Facilitated Small Groups | Cooperative Groups | Pairs | Individuals |
|---|---|---|---|---|---|
| Teacher Read-Aloud | √ | √ | | | |
| Demonstrations | √ | √ | | | |
| Readers' Theatre/Story Theatre | √ | √ | | | |
| Rereading with Taped Story | | | | √ | √ |
| Buddy Reading | | | | √ | |
| Support for Emergent or Struggling Readers | | √ | | | |
| Journals | √ | | | √ | √ |
| Literature Circles | | | √ | | |
| Self-Selected Reading | | | | √ | √ |
| Projects | √ | | √ | √ | √ |
| Conferencing | | | | √ | √ |
| Direct Instruction | √ | √ | | | |
| Author's Chair | √ | | √ | | |
| Learning Centers | | | √ | √ | √ |

# Pacing Literacy Instruction:
## An Interview with Dr. W. Dorsey Hammond

Dr. Hammond, Professor of Education at Oakland University in Rochester, Michigan, answers some questions teachers often ask about the pacing of instruction.

**Q** I often wonder if my pacing of instruction is appropriate. Are there some basic guidelines I can use?

**A** Pacing of instruction is something we must constantly monitor. Every thoughtful teacher wonders about it. "Am I moving the instruction too quickly or too slowly?" "Am I trying to do too much?" "Am I leaving out some important skills or strategies?" and so on.

Only the individual teacher can make these decisions. The basic guideline is that our children must be involved in learning experiences that are challenging enough for new learning to occur but not so difficult that children are overwhelmed and begin to be afraid or withdraw. Conversely, the material and learning experiences must not be so easy that children aren't learning anything new and become bored. Reading teachers think about the appropriate match between learners and the learning activities as the "instructional level," or "range."

**Q** I am using a program that provides several activities and lessons for each selection in the children's textbook. Do I have to do everything?

**A** The key here is to be selective. There won't be time for you to do everything. Nor is it necessary. You may decide, for example, to omit certain activities or even to be selective in the stories the children read.

**Q** Why are there so many activities and stories if I'm not expected to do them all?

**A** So you will have choice. Just as when you go into a library, a bookstore, or even a grocery store, you choose what you want and need or what your children want and need. This is not to suggest that you should skip too much—it is just that you can make informed decisions.

**Q** If I skip a story in the textbook, won't the children miss out on some of the skills?

**A** All of the stories in a carefully planned literature program are worth reading, and each contributes to your children's reading growth. However, the skills and strategies are so carefully interwoven and repeated throughout the fabric of the entire program that you can comfortably be a bit selective.

In addition to choosing *what* your children read, you will need to make some decisions about *how* they read. You will choose to have children read some selections with your guidance and direction so that you can model good reading strategies. Other selections may be read independently by all children or by a portion of your class. Still other selections may be read and discussed by a literature circle or other subgroup of your class.

**You mentioned grouping. I have a wide range of reading abilities in my primary classroom. Should I have reading groups in different books?**

 This is really a district or individual school decision made at the local level. Research tells us that children in the "low group" seldom grow or achieve well enough to get out of the low group. Students really do need opportunities to work with others who are at different achievement levels.

If the text is too difficult for some students, you may choose to read some or all of the story to the less-able readers and then have them practice repeated readings. Or they may listen to the selection on a tape and follow along in their text. In addition, make sure the less-able readers are selecting and reading library books they can read independently with much success.

Encourage students to read as well as they can even if a story is very challenging. Accept their best efforts.

 **I have twenty-six students in my intermediate class. Should all of them be reading the same story at the same time?**

 In some cases, all students could be reading the same story. However, it is not easy for twenty-six students to have a discussion at the same time. Some students just don't get a chance to share their ideas and opinions. Thus, you may elect to have half your class read and discuss the selection at one time and the other half at another time. Or some students may read it independently. Another alternative is to establish literature circles in your classroom, with each circle responding to the story. With modeling and practice, intermediate students are quite capable of monitoring their own behavior as they respond to a story with several of their peers.

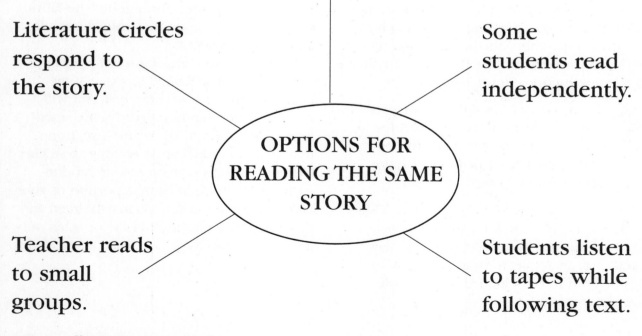

Half the class reads and discusses the story at a time.

Literature circles respond to the story.

Some students read independently.

OPTIONS FOR READING THE SAME STORY

Teacher reads to small groups.

Students listen to tapes while following text.

**I never seem to have enough time to do all I want to do. Do you have any recommendations?**

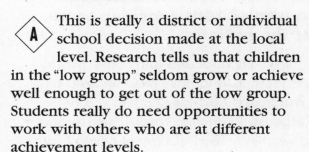 Really good teachers are always saying, "If I just had more time." It is part of our profession. It seems we are always adding something to the curriculum but never taking anything out.

Here are three things we can do to save time and increase our efficiency:

1. Think about a school day and ask yourself," "What did we do today that didn't seem to make a difference?" Do this for a few days, and you will probably find some activities that aren't worth the time you spend on them. In other words, clean up your school day and throw out what isn't needed.

2. Establish with students rituals of getting underway, moving from one activity to another, settling down in the morning or after lunch, taking out and putting away materials, and so on. As we find 30 seconds here and 30 seconds there, it soon adds up to a few minutes a day that can be used to read a few extra pages to your students or allow them to read or write for a few more minutes.

3. Look for activities that increase student interaction, such as cooperative learning. Have students read to one another in small groups rather than having one student read and twenty-five students listen. Involve students in choral and echo reading. Allow students to help one another, thus reinforcing and promoting language interaction.

Finally, accept that the pacing of instruction will always be an issue with many dimensions. There is no one prescription. Trust your own judgment and the judgment of your colleagues.

**I have a wide range of reading abilities in my classroom. Should I have reading groups in different books?**

This is really a district or individual school decision made at the local level. Research tells us that children in the "low group" seldom grow or achieve well enough to get out of the low group. Students really do need opportunities to work with others who are at different achievement levels.

# Journaling

by Dr. Donna M. Ogle
Chair, Reading and Language Department,
National-Louis University, Evanston, Illinois

## How can teachers best use journals? Let's consider some of the options.

First, a natural and fairly easy way to use journals is to have children keep a **Literature Log** (or Reading Log or Response Journal) to record their responses to what they read. (Different types of journals are called by a number of different names. The labels themselves, of course, are less important than the techniques.) The log can simply be a notebook in which children record the day they are writing, the title of the book they are reading, and their thoughts and feelings about what they have just read. They can respond in any way, but some guiding questions can be helpful, especially at first. For example:

What stands out most about the section you just read? What do you like best about this part?

What images, or pictures, came to mind while you read?

How do you feel about the characters? Why?

What questions came to mind as you read? Was there any part you didn't understand or didn't like?

What do you think is going to happen next in the story?

Some teachers also have students include at the back of the log a running list of all the books and articles they read. This gives both the teacher and the students a way of evaluating the range of their reading, the challenge of the materials, and the possibilities for future selections.

A natural extension of the Literature Log is a **Dialogue Journal.** In this type of journal, the teacher responds to what the child has written. Teacher responses can extend what the child has noted, can raise questions for deeper reflection ("Why do you suppose the character acted that way?" or "What would you have done in that situation?"), and can help the child enjoy the process of writing, by providing a real audience for his or her comments.

Some teachers find that responding to students' journals takes a great deal of time. The choice to use **Buddy Journals** for some of the year may provide a welcome change. With Buddy Journals, children become partners and share their journals, reading and responding to each other's comments and reflections. Students will work better as partners if they have already had experience with teacher-student Dialogue Journals. Discussion and modeling of what is appropriate in dialogue is important. The class can compose a list of the kinds of comments that are appropriate. These might include:

- what I liked in your entry
- a connection I made to my experience or to another book I read
- a question asking for more information
- a suggestion for additional reading

Two other forms of journaling are also valuable in the intermediate classroom. **Daily Journals** help students learn to write about their own experiences and thoughts. Many teachers have students keep spiral notebooks in their desks and use the first few moments of the day or of the class to put their own thinking on paper. In addition, if some class members get upset or involved in an argument, the teacher can turn to the journals and let each child write out his or her feelings.

Teachers can also have students use Daily Journals as the starting point for more structured writing. Ideas that students are thinking about can be saved for elaboration later. Suggestions for writing prompts can be developed by the class. Here are some examples:

- Reflect on what you are learning and how you are learning it.
- Explain what things you are most interested in currently and keep a record so you can know yourself better.
- What are your goals for today?

Students can also use journals for saving interesting phrases, descriptions, and words that they encounter in reading and in other contexts. Through the use of such **Learning Logs,** students become more attuned to their environment and begin to learn from it in new ways. This writing time, whenever used, can also help settle students and let them focus on learning.

Learning Logs can enhance content-area learning. At the end of each class session or after a few days of concentrated learning, ask students to write their reflections on what they have learned. They might track the progress of science experiments. Encourage them to use charts and other visuals where appropriate. You may want to start with questions like these:

- What did you learn that was the most interesting?
- What surprised you the most about what you learned?
- How was your class participation? Did you help the group?
- What questions do you have as a result of what you have learned?
- What other sources of information could be useful as we learn more?

**Character or History Diaries** can help students make connections between themselves and the content they are studying. When children are asked to reflect on how they would have felt or what they might have done during historical periods or in particular situations, the content can come to life. Putting themselves in the shoes of a period character can focus students' thinking and make the content much more enjoyable. When studying about the Colonial period, for example, a child can write as a Tory or as a Patriot child.

Whatever the content, journaling can enhance learning. When children share their writing, the whole class can benefit.

**Q** **How do I get started with primary children?**

 **A** Construct individual journals for children with primary paper that has space for drawing and writing. Write, or have children write, their names on the covers and then let them illustrate the covers. One teacher made journals a family affair by asking family members to design covers for blank journals when they came for an initial parents' night. When children received their journals with drawings and messages from their parents, the whole purpose of journaling was clear and the joy immediate!

**Q** **How do the youngest children write in their journals?**

**A** Even when they start kindergarten, many children bring with them the ability to write some words, especially their names. Find out what they can write by asking them to write all the words they know in their journals. Or ask them to write about what they want to learn in school or about favorite animals, foods, TV shows, and so on.

Children can draw responses to these queries even if they can't write the individual words. As children draw, you can circulate with small slips of paper to write the full messages children want. Give them the slips of paper to paste in their journals. In this way you will have a permanent record of children's intended writing.

Many primary children find writing to be slow and laborious. Help these children enjoy journaling by encouraging them to construct entries in other ways. They can share ideas by drawing pictures of what they think is important. They can cut out text and illustrations from magazines that help communicate their ideas and then paste these in their journals. When you create class messages and news updates, make copies for children to include in their journals. Some of the most creative and useful journals I've seen in primary grades were created from a variety of media.

**Q** **How can I help children use the journal productively?**

**A** Some teachers like to provide time at the end of the day for writing in a group journal. By bringing the children together and asking them to think about the day's events, you nurture the habit of reflection. Write children's contributions in the class journal, including their names by what they said.

One teacher noted a dramatic difference in her children when she used group journaling. They took more notice of what the class was doing. At an open house, several parents seemed particularly surprised and pleased. One explained, "When we ask Sara what happens in school, she now can tell us specific events. Before, she would just shrug and tell us she couldn't remember."

**Q** **How often should children write in their journals?**

**A** If daily journaling seems like too much, then take time once or twice a week to reflect with the group. Sometimes a group discussion can stimulate children to return to their desks and write. Each teacher needs to find what works best for a particular group. You can try alternating a day of group journaling with a day of individual journaling. Remember that when journals are kept at their desks, children are more likely to use them. Since some will "take to" journaling more than others, encourage this approach.

# Reader Response

## by Dr. Karen Kutiper

English Language Arts Consultant, Harris County Department of Education, Houston, Texas

When Tanya writes in her journal, "I felt like I was really living in the town," and Jason writes, "At the end I felt calm and peaceful," we know that Byrd Baylor's *The Best Town in the World* has aroused in these young readers personal, emotional connections between what they read and their own worlds. Their responses go beyond story recall or the retelling of story parts. They have personalized their reading, and their reading experiences will somehow change or enhance the way they think and the way they react to texts in the future.

Reader response theory tells us that meaning comes from *both* the reader and the text. Today we equate the term *reader response* with an approach to reading that increases readers' personal involvement with literature and that complements, enhances, or sometimes replaces more traditional approaches to reading instruction that have focused mainly on the text. Rather than just learning *about* a piece of literature, readers in a response-based classroom *experience* it. They have an important, active role in determining the meaning of what they read, and they connect their own life experiences to their understanding of the literature.

Whether experiences with literature occur as read-alouds by the teacher, self-selected or teacher-assigned reading, sustained silent reading, or partner or small-group reading of the same selection, we can guide and support reader response in several ways:

- through the use of open-ended questions that promote personal connections,
- through reader response groups organized to promote literature discussion,
- through informal writing opportunities.

## Questions

If we want to encourage personal response, we first need to examine the types of questions that we use to initiate and guide discussions about literature. Whether in small-group or whole-group discussion, the questions or prompts that encourage talking about books in a response-based classroom focus not on single right answers but on students choosing how to respond. Questions like "What did you think about this book?" or "Did this book remind you of another book you have read?" focus on individual responses and personal connections. Research has shown that questions that encourage students to focus on the "lived-through" experience of reading tend to elicit high-level responses. That is, some questions should address students' thoughts and feelings *during* reading; for example, "Did your feelings about the main character change as you read the book?"

## Reader Response Groups

Reader response groups are small groups of students responding to literature in a supportive, collaborative environment. Often called book clubs, literature study groups, or literature circles, these groups provide a comfortable format for discussion. Student dialogue, not teacher talk, is the crucial ingredient in a response group. While we can organize and schedule these groups in a variety of ways, their focus is usually on providing a structure that will allow readers to explore personal meanings and deepen critical understandings. As group members become accustomed to making their own choices and initiating their own discussions, the teacher can allow the groups more autonomy.

## Informal Writing

Informal writing about literature helps students reflect both on the literature and on themselves and their personal responses to a selection. Formats for informal writing might include written conversations (J. Harste, K. G. Short, C. Burke, 1988), dialogue journals (N. Atwell, 1987), and literature logs or literature response journals.

"**Reader response theory tells us that meaning comes from both the reader and the text.**"

Whether informal written responses are guided by open-ended questions or probes or consist entirely of free writing, they can help readers "see" what they think about a literature selection. Because students feel as though they have something to share, reading aloud these written responses can also become a way to begin group discussion.

The results of a focus on reader response and the use of classroom strategies that promote personal engagement are many. Students increase their ability to reflect on their reading, and they deepen their understandings. They come to acknowledge and appreciate different perspectives, which sometimes leads to rethinking and revising their initial responses. They think critically and creatively about their reading. When we both honor and facilitate personal responses to literature, we foster greater understanding, increased appreciation, and a lifelong love of reading.

# CONFERENCING TO
# DIRECT STUDENTS' STRATEGY DEVELOPMENT

## by Dr. Roger C. Farr

Chancellor's Professor of Education and Director of the Center for Reading and Language Studies, Indiana University

The methodology that ensures a link between assessment and instruction is the use of student-teacher conferences. Individual conferences have the advantage of allowing a student to benefit from focused teacher attention, and they usually encourage more open and candid discussions. On the other hand, small-group conferences allow students to learn from one another.

## The Goals of Strategy Conferences

Regardless of the format, the goal of a strategy conference is to help students recognize their own strengths and the areas in which they need development. Most importantly, the conferences should focus on reading and writing about students' genuine interests,

informational needs, and desires to create and to communicate with particular audiences. Regular strategy conferences help students synthesize what they have learned about language use.

## Preparing for Conferences

Students should prepare for a strategy conference by thinking about what they have read, what they enjoyed about the reading, and what purposes the reading served. At the same time, students should already have made some self-analysis of their writing for the period; they should review the targeted audiences for various pieces of writing, the purposes they had for writing each piece, and how effectively the writing served the purpose. This ongoing

self-analysis is naturally encouraged by having students keep logs of what they read and write, including their personal reactions and comments about both the text and the strategies they used. Developing students' self-assessment skills is particularly easy in classrooms where the students keep *portfolios*.

Since much that students write stems from the background created by reading, some teachers have students keep a single log that combines reading and writing experiences and demonstrates in the sequence of its entries how reading and writing interact. There are, as well, numerous types of simple records that promote open-ended self-analysis of reading, writing, and strategy development.

While the teacher may also prepare by reviewing the various formal and informal assessments she or he has kept for each student, the teacher's analysis should not overpower self-analysis by the student. As students spend time regularly considering their use of language, they will become more adept at discussing personal progress with the teacher in each successive conference. At the same time, students will be more prepared to articulate personal goals for strategy development after the conference. The students should keep a record of these goals so that conferences can begin by reviewing the goals and considering what has been accomplished in achieving them. Questions such as those on page 25 can help students think about the strategies they use.

## Scheduling Conferences

Try to schedule at least four strategy conferences during the school year. These conferences can be a combination of individual and small-group conferences. The object of conferencing is to develop in each student a genuine sense of being a reader and a writer, to appreciate how those and other language activities serve authentic life interests, and to encourage self-assessment, so that lifelong development of useful language strategies continues.

## During a Strategy Conference

It is not a good idea to attempt to focus on too many strategies in one conference. You may decide, for example, to emphasize only two or three strategies in your first conferences. Your questions and your discussions with students would revolve around those strategies. For example, to focus on using background knowledge, you might ask students to tell you about what they already knew about a story they read or wrote and ask them to talk about how what they already knew made the story more interesting.

A form that you can use as part of the conference appears on page 26. This form lists eight strategies and provides room for both the teacher and the student to write their ideas about the student's reading and writing performance.

# Questions for Self-Assessing Strategy Use

| Strategies Used | ESSENTIAL BEHAVIORS IN READING AND WRITING |
|---|---|
| set purpose | **1.** *What was my purpose for reading/writing this? What did I want to know or want my audience to know?* |
| access background knowledge | **2.** *Do I think about what I already know about a topic before I begin to read or to write about it?* |
| prediction (before) | **3.** *Do I think ahead about what might happen in a story or about what I want to write?* |
| prediction (during) | **4.** *Do I predict what is coming next while I am reading or think about what will come next while I am writing?* |
| visualization | **5.** *Do I picture in my mind what I am reading about or telling about in my writing?* |
| metacognition | **6.** *When I am reading or writing, do I ask myself whether what I am reading or writing makes good sense?* |
| revision | **7.** *Do I change my mind about what I am learning as I read or about what I am saying as I write? Do I make changes if things aren't making good sense?* |
| self-assessment | **8.** *Do I get help when I need it? Do I reread or ask the teacher or a friend for help?* |

## Conference Notes

Name _____

Date _____

| ? What do I know? | Predict before? | Predict during? | Picture? | Make Sense? | Make changes? | Get help? |
|---|---|---|---|---|---|---|
| Purpose | | | | | | |

**Teacher's Notes**

**Student's Notes**

# A *QUICK* REFERENCE GUIDE *to* TEACHING STRATEGIES

### By Dr. W. Dorsey Hammond
**Professor in Reading and Language Arts, Oakland University, Rochester, Michigan**

Even as competent educators, we sometimes need an additional strategy to use; or perhaps we need to be reminded of a workable strategy that we may have overlooked. Below are ten challenging teaching and learning situations. Each situation is accompanied by teaching strategies that are usually successful in improving the learning behavior.

| PROBLEM/SITUATION | CONSIDERATIONS | SUGGESTED STRATEGIES |
|---|---|---|
| **Good word recognition but poor comprehension.** | Student may view reading only as a "sounding out" process and needs to see reading also as a meaning process.<br><br>Student may not be reading with a strong purpose or using enough prior knowledge. | Make sure students begin by assessing their prior knowledge *before* reading.<br><br>Have students predict what the story will be about or what they will learn.<br><br>Just before students read, ask them to tell you what they expect to find out or what questions they have.<br><br>Use a think-aloud process to model for students how you think when you read.<br><br>Use K-W-L and other student-centered strategies. |
| **Lacks confidence as a reader.** | This is characteristic of many students who are experiencing difficulty in learning to read. | Use materials with which students can find success. In early stages of learning to read, use predictable books, stories, environmental print activities, and so on.<br><br>Use the Repeated Reading strategy on selected pages (See Glossary of Professional Terms.) |
| **When reading orally, student seems not to understand the text.** | It is very difficult to simultaneously read aloud in front of classmates and understand unfamiliar text. The reader's attention is on being fluent and avoiding mistakes and not necessarily on construction meaning. | Encourage silent reading before oral reading.<br><br>Allow students to practice alone or with a partner before reading to a group.<br><br>Remember that reading aloud with classmates is not primarily for comprehension but for the purpose of sharing the story or listening to the beauty of the language. |
| **Reading silently and not comprehending.** | Focused and motivated silent reading is an important skill to develop.<br><br>Some students, when reading silently, appear to allow their minds to wander, or read passively, or, in some cases, merely pretend to read. | Encourage many predictions about what will happen next in the story.<br><br>For informational text, encourage students to predict the answers to their questions.<br><br>Have students pause more often after reading to summarize what they have read and revise their predictions.<br><br>Have students declare their own purposes for reading.<br><br>Encourage students to keep a response journal in which to write briefly what they are thinking as they are reading. |

| PROBLEM/SITUATION | CONSIDERATIONS | SUGGESTED STRATEGIES |
|---|---|---|
| **Has difficulty recognizing words in the text or story.** | Remember, the best way to improve word recognition is to do a great deal of reading—even reading a favorite story over and over again.<br><br>Context (making sense), phonics, and language ability all contribute to word recognition. | Encourage students to predict what word would make sense.<br><br>Start with beginning sounds and then go on to rhyming patterns to facilitate recognition.<br><br>Have the student look for parts of words that he or she already knows.<br><br>Discuss other strategies students might use. |
| **Word-by-word reading; lack of fluency.** | Student may lack confidence.<br>Student may be relying exclusively on sounding out words.<br>Reading material may be too difficult.<br>Student may not be using prior knowledge to interact with the text. | Use Repeated Readings.<br>Use choral and echo reading with favorite poems and other selections with predictable language.<br>Switch to easier reading material.<br>Encourage students to think about what they already know about the topic or story *before* they begin reading. |
| **Appears to disregard punctuation when reading.** | Disregarding punctuation is usually an effect of *not* comprehending. As students improve in comprehension, their intuitive sense of punctuation also improves. | Read a passage (with inflection) to students. Have them tell you when to punctuate and what punctuation to use.<br><br>On an overhead, provide students with a passage of two or three paragraphs that have not been punctuated. Have students work cooperatively in groups of two to punctuate the passage. |
| **Student looks at the initial letter and then guesses at the word, with little attention to the remainder of the word.** | A certain amount of guessing is helpful. However, student may be feeling undue pressure and thus looks at the first letter and produces the first word that comes to mind. | When students are reading in context, encourage them to think about what word would make sense.<br><br>Have student read a short list of words all beginning with the same letter. Examples: *red, reach, ready, reply, reason; money, Monday, monkey, motion, moment.* Such activities will gently force the student to look beyond the first letter and attend to the rest of the word. |
| **Student has difficulty reading an entire book.** | Students are sometimes intimidated by the prospect of reading an entire novel for the first time.<br><br>Often it is the reluctant reader or the reader who is least confident who has difficulty sustaining himself or herself through a novel. | Make sure the student has selected a novel in an area of interest.<br>Check for appropriateness of difficulty level.<br>Look for a novel that has a fast-paced story. Confer with the student from time to time, discussing what has happened in the story and asking him or her to predict what will happen next.<br>Give the reader a break by reading a chapter to the student or by having a parent read a chapter.<br>Implement a Sustained Reading program in your classroom to increase the amount of time students are able to read without interruption. |
| **Has difficulty selecting appropriate books from library.** | Students are often at a loss when asked to select books they will enjoy and find meaningful.<br><br>Some students will often pick books that are too easy or too difficult. Other students will only read books by the same author or from the same series. | Begin by discussing students' interests. Talk about favorite authors students have read before. Suggest revisiting some of these authors.<br><br>Encourage students to browse through books, reading a page or two of each before choosing.<br><br>Encourage students to take risks by reading a new author or a different kind of story. |

© Harcourt

# INTEGRATING THE LANGUAGE ARTS

**BY DR. DOROTHY S. STRICKLAND**
**The State of New Jersey Professor of Reading, Ruters University**

*The language arts—listening, speaking, reading, and writing—are interrelated, and they should be taught that way. Although some individual lessons focus on one or the other of the language arts, every opportunity should be taken to reinforce and strengthen all of them as an integrated whole. Below are some tips for integrating listening, speaking, reading, and writing in the classroom:*

## INTEGRATING
## WRITING
### WITH READING, LISTENING, AND SPEAKING

- Group writing projects should be posted at a convenient level for students to read on their own.
- Student-authored books may be bound and placed in the classroom library along with commercially published materials.
- Student-authored materials may be read aloud for listening and response by the whole group or by a small group.
- Student-authored materials, fiction or nonfiction, may be tape-recorded for others to enjoy and to gain information from.

## INTEGRATING
## LISTENING
### WITH READING, WRITING, AND SPEAKING

- Use group writing conferences to have students listen to a work in progress and offer thoughtful suggestions to the writer.
- Critical listening to a story containing an important life theme allows students to form opinions for discussion.
- Use a work with a repetitive refrain or an interesting pattern as a model for children to follow in writing their own works. A good book to select is *If You Give a Mouse a Cookie* by Laura Joffee Numeroff (HarperCollins, 1985).

## INTEGRATING
## S P E A K I N G

### WITH LISTENING, READING, AND WRITING

- Encourage students to use informal talk about a topic as preparation for writing or for giving a formal report. Speaking and writing are both expressive processes. They both require the ability to select significant ideas and organize them with clarity and a sense of audience.

- Have students give "book talks" on books they have read, and then have them encourage response by asking for questions and comments from the group.

- Have children read a descriptive paragraph and then paraphrase it.

- Encourage children to describe, using vivid language and sensory details, something they like to do or some place they have been. Have listeners respond by telling what they liked about the description and what they visualized as the speaker talked.

- Use discussion to stimulate further reading. After discussion, students may list the things they want to learn more about. This should be followed by reading and sharing.

## INTEGRATING
## R E A D I N G

### WITH WRITING, LISTENING, AND SPEAKING

- Expose children to a wide variety of fiction and nonfiction, and discuss the text features. These features serve as models for children's writing.

- Read aloud frequently, and engage students in a variety of means of response. Reading and listening are both receptive processes dependent upon comprehension and interpretation.

Here are some ideas for responding:

✓ Have students draw their favorite parts.

✓ Organize students into pairs or small groups to act out their favorite scenes.

✓ Have students write what they think will happen next and then share it with a partner. Have partners respond to each other's predictions.

✓ Have students retell the story or a part of the story in their own words.

✓ Have students read aloud their written reports on topics under study. Listeners may respond by asking questions and by sharing what they learned.

✓ Poetry is meant to be read aloud. Students may collect favorite poems and take turns reading them aloud to the group. This is best done two or three at a time over a period of weeks.

# ACTIVITIES THAT INTEGRATE READING STRATEGIES

The strategies you want your students to command are not separate, artificial performances. They are interrelated and interdependent, because they are aimed at one goal: constructing meaning. In an effective reading and writing classroom, students develop strategies in meaningful contexts, as they communicate ideas with their teachers and their peers. Let's take a look at some of the strategy-building activities you might find in an effective classroom.

## Shared Reading

Many strategies and skills are modeled as teacher and students work together to read a text. Students have an opportunity to "try out" what they know in a risk-free environment. Teachers can highlight reading strategies during shared reading by modeling making predictions, noting details, identifying cause and effect, and summarizing.

## Response Journals

Students may respond to a prompt given by the teacher or offer a free response. Here is an example of a teacher prompt: Think about the two main characters, Jacqueline and Jon. Tell how they are alike and how they are different. Then explain which character you would rather meet, and why. To respond, students must (1) recall relevant details, (2) compare and contrast, (3) make inferences, and (4) form and express judgments. All are key comprehension strategies.

## Dialogue Journals

In an effective outgrowth of journal writing, each student maintains a one-to-one written conversation with the teacher. The conversation may be held in a separate journal or in a designated section of a journal the student uses for several purposes. Students write to the teacher about what they have read, what they think about their reading, or anything else they want to share. At regular intervals, perhaps once a week, the teacher collects students' dialogue journals and writes brief, encouraging responses.

## Book Discussion Groups

After reading, discussion frequently centers on the responses students have made in their journals. When students read aloud from their journals, teachers have an opportunity to learn how they have internalized strategies and expressed their own ideas. During discussion, students have an opportunity to draw on all their strategies for reading. Some of the strategies exercised in meaningful discussions are making judgments, identifying main ideas, classifying information, and drawing conclusions.

## Literature Mapping

Mapping stories at even the simplest levels allows students to reorganize information and classify it into key components. For example, the teacher gives each student a large piece of construction paper divided into six to eight boxes and has the students label each box using the following categories: general information (title, author, illustrator); main characters (the name of each in a separate box; students fill in information and ideas about each character); favorite part; interesting language; setting; recommendation; and so on. Students fill in each box with appropriate words and sometimes pictures. The categories to be used can be determined by the teacher and student together. This activity requires students to recall information, categorize ideas, retell events, describe, explain, and evaluate.

## Oral Reading

One-to-one conferences and literature discussion groups offer the teacher opportunities to listen to students read aloud selected portions of text. The teacher can use this time to observe students' command of strategies from the following perspectives:

• Is the reading fluent? Smooth reading indicates good comprehension.

• Is appropriate intonation used? Inappropriate intonation or a lack of expressiveness during oral reading may mean the student does not understand what is being pronounced.

• Does the student self-correct to preserve meaning? This indicates that the student is monitoring his or her reading.

• Does the student take risks in the pronunciation of unknown words? A child who feels confident about using phonics together with context clues will usually give an unknown word a reasonable try. The attempts children make give us a great deal of information about the way they are processing text.

Through modeling and discussion, the teacher can help students apply the following strategies when they confront unknown words:

– Read ahead for more context clues.
– Reread to see what might make sense and whether anything was missed.
– Use picture clues.
– Use the first letters of the word as a clue.
– If the word is too troublesome and does not seem important to the meaning, skip it and continue reading.

© Harcourt

# Real-Life Reading

## by Dr. Donna M. Ogle

Chair, Reading and Language Arts
Department, National Louis University

*Build bridges between your students' classroom reading and their out-of-school experiences.*

The more students handle and browse through various materials, the more intrigued they will become with reading. Unfortunately, many kids don't have newspapers and magazines in their homes.

**TIP 1** – Keep newspapers, magazines, and catalogs in a browsing corner.

- Invite students to use the material to find information about topics they are studying.

- Use a weather map to find out the climate and weather in the part of the world you are reading about in literature or social studies.

- Find pictures that illustrate special concepts or characters about whom the class is studying or reading.

- Have students fill out catalog order forms for items your group selects. Students can check each other's work to see if they completed the order forms correctly.

**TIP 2** – Collect old telephone books. Use them to focus on real-life reading activities.

- Use the yellow pages to help students with categorization. Write specific items or services on the board to see if students can locate the correct category. You might want to list the name of a drugstore, medical doctor, local bus company, city government office, local school superintendent's office, and so on. Discuss how we organize by a larger category and by subcategories. This is a good lesson to transfer to all student learning.

- The telephone directory also can be used to teach spelling and variations in spelling. Have students work in pairs to locate names and phone numbers that you select. Names beginning with *Mc* or abbreviations such as *U.S.* or *St.* can illustrate the need to understand systems of alphabetizing.

**TIP 3** – Develop careful reading.

- Reading guides for TV programs, computer software, and local events is both important and fun. Provide student partners with a challenge list. For example, they might find the times for an upcoming sports event, compare the programs at 9:00 P.M. on two local television stations, find the best 6:00 P.M. radio station programs, or determine which computers have the best features for the classroom's needs.

**TIP 4** – Stress the importance of giving and following directions.

- Careful reading is important for students in the middle grades. Use special school functions or annual events to develop careful reading habits. Have students construct holiday decorations or make origami gifts. Locate books that provide step-by-step directions that students must follow for success.

- Students can plan a field trip, including a schedule, directions, and transportation, and follow their own plans.

- Use real road maps and provide directions to reach a specific destination. Students who plan a trip and then write the directions to the destination can improve their oral communication skills.

# Integrating Technology

*Special thanks to Dr. Shelley B. Wepner and Dr. Nancy E. Seminoff for their help in developing this article.*

T**oday's** students do not have to go very far to experience the excitement of the Information Age. Cyber-learning activities for students dazzle the senses as different constructs, strategies, and materials are used to promote literacy. Although debates abound about the place of technological "edutainment" in the classroom, technology certainly can contribute to student's literacy development if it functions as part of good curriculum planning. In creating these plans, we need to consider the concepts and content that we want students to acquire, the materials we will use, and the organization of activities. These considerations determine how we will choose software and appropriate Internet Web sites, and how we will organize our classrooms and our time.

**"Cyber-learning activities for students dazzle the senses..."**

## Software

Successful integration begins with choosing technology products that blend with the lessons and skills covered in the classroom. In selecting software as one type of interactivity, consider these suggestions:

- Select software that supports your curriculum plan. If you use trade books, consider electronic collections in which the entire contents of popular books appear to come alive on-screen. Use the materials referenced in teacher's editions to introduce, reinforce, or extend a lesson.

- Become familiar with the software you select. Explore the versatility and flexibility of the products you have.

- Choose software that supports—directly or by extension—literature-based plans, content-area learning, and thematic units.

- Motivate students by identifying age-appropriate software. There are many different word processing applications made specifically for elementary students that offer text processing, paint programs, and text-to-speech capabilities.

- Know whether the package is most appropriate for an initial introduction to a large group, a small group, or an individual, and whether it lends itself to teacher-student collaboration or student-student collaboration.

- Provide students with programs that promote the exploration of information. CD-ROM encyclopedias enable users to browse with ease and explore information in both a linear and nonlinear way. Many DVD products allow students to experience and manipulate information through a variety of activities.

## Connecting Your Classroom

Connect your class to the Internet. In selecting online Internet activities, consider these suggestions:

- Practice Web safety. Before students venture onto the cyber-superhighway, they should complete an "Internet Safety Rules" worksheet. Remind students that the important online rules are:
  **1.** never give out private information;
  **2.** never agree to meet in person;
  **3.** always tell an adult if inappropriate content appears on-screen;
  **4.** always understand which sites are allowed and which are off-limits; and
  **5.** follow the same rules whether at school, in the library, or at home.

- Join a "teacher's only" list-serv or electronic bulletin board to receive and exchange helpful classroom ideas. These free services are generally organized by grade level or topic, and they can provide hundreds of online lesson plans, class projects, and suggested links.

- "Surf the Web" for innovative, cross-curricular, or theme-related sites; allowing you to direct students effectively and safely to those Web sites that enhance or extend your text-based lesson plans.

- Explore ways for students to create documents that link Internet resources with their research. Post cooperative research reports on your school's Web site or other free Internet posting sites to share with others.

- Motivate your class to explore additional information hypertextually. For example, while reading a selection based on sea turtles, students could go online to see a video clip of a turtle returning to sea, hear a narration by a marine scientist, or take a virtual trip to the Galapagos Islands.

- Visit the publisher's Web site of the textbooks you use to extend, enhance, and enrich the text-based curriculum. Many publishers place references to their Web activities in teacher's guide at points of use.

## Organizing Your Classroom

Whether you have one computer, a computer lab in the library, or a computer for every student, you have many ways to successfully integrate technology into your lesson plan. To make the most of your available software applications and hardware (monitors, disk drives, printers, and so on), consider these suggestions:

- Try to arrange for the use of projection devices such as large-screen monitors and LCD (Liquid Crystal Display) panels so that a large group of students can watch one large monitor.

- Bargain with other teachers to borrow additional computers for a specified time.

- Help students identify other locations in the community or school where computers are available.

- Create a daily and weekly schedule.

- Use a learning-center approach so that while some students are working on a computer project, other students are working on a different project.

- Group two to four students for projects. Pair students who are computer literate with students who are not.

- Use an aide or a parent volunteer to assist students.

## and more . . .

- Attend local, statewide, and national computer-oriented conferences, or technology-related workshops.

- Subscribe to technology magazines and journals for information on topics such as software, hardware, and lesson plans.

- Ask PTAs and other groups involved with the school to secure additional hardware and software through grants and philanthropic organizations.

Identify the methods that work best for you and your students. Find the appropriate "technology to text" mixture for continued literacy growth and functional integrated learning.

# Using
# THEMATIC UNITS TO FACILITATE LEARNING

BY PATRICIA SMITH

Elementary Reading/Language Arts Coordinator, Cypress-Fairbanks School District, Houston, Texas
and Adjunct Professor of Education, University of Houston, Clear Lake City

Here are some questions many teachers ask about thematic units:

## How do students profit when learning takes place within a thematic organization?

- Connections are formed among concepts that students may have seen as unrelated.
- Skills are learned in a meaningful context.
- Vocabulary and concepts are developed and solidified through repeated usage over time.
- Choices within the unit offer students ownership of their learning.
- Opportunities for learning within a community are plentiful.
- Learning time is maximized, because multiple subjects are integrated.
- Learners are motivated by real-life connections in the theme and by opportunities for a variety of activities.

## What are some common ways themes are organized within the classroom?

Here are some common organizational patterns, with examples.

| Organizational Pattern | Example | Content |
|---|---|---|
| Topic | Environment | Literature and experiences about the environment |
| Concept | Individuals can make the world more beautiful. | Literature and experiences about beauty, art, nature, and individual growth |
| Genre | Biographies | Biographies and experiences to learn about a variety of people |
| Author | Beverly Cleary | Literature and experiences to explore books by Beverly Cleary |

## How can I plan for thematic instruction?

- Choose a theme that is broad enough to support many connections.
- Determine process and content objectives.
- Decide how much time will be spent, keeping in mind the need to be flexible in responding to students' interests and needs.
- Gather resources such as literature, reference materials, videotapes, audiocassettes, software, artifacts, and information about possible guest speakers. Some materials and ideas should come from students.
- Decide what kinds of learning experiences you want students to have. One way to plan the learning is to use a framework like the following:

| Type of Experience | Initiating | Ongoing | Culminating |
|---|---|---|---|
| **Purpose** | Motivates<br>Activates back-<br>  ground knowledge<br>Sets the focus | Engages the learner<br>  in authentic reading,<br>  writing, listening,<br>  and speaking | Summarizes<br>Synthesizes<br>Determines direction<br>  for further learning |

- Next, determine which learning experiences will be conducted independently, in student pairs, in small cooperative groups, and with the whole class.
- Determine the evaluation measures. This usually involves a combination of assessment techniques, such as informal observation, running records, student and teacher portfolios for each student, and literature-based skill activities evaluated through performance assessment. (See also the "Assessment" section of this guide.)

## Tips for planning thematic units:

**1.** Ask yourself whether your thematic unit

- contains quality fiction and nonfiction literature.
- provides material on a variety of reading levels.
- offers opportunities for authentic reading, writing, listening, and speaking.
- provides for further development of strategic reading and writing.
- forms natural links to other curriculum areas.
- offers opportunities for choice.
- provides opportunities for students to experience membership in a community of learners.

**2.** Use a flowchart like the following, filling in the specific information for your chosen unit.

| Complete the shared literature experiences to initiate the unit. |

↓

| Use a K-W-L chart to determine what students know and what they want to know about the topic. |

↓

| Form groups of students with shared interests to explore the questions listed in the "W" column of the K-W-L chart. |

↓

| Encourage daily small-group and self-evaluations on the inquiry progress and collaboration efforts. |

↓

| Arrange for sharing the information learned. |

↓

| Add new information to the "L" column of the K-W-L chart. |

↓

| Help students determine directions for self-directed future learning on the topic. |

**3.** Work with other teachers as much as possible to plan the thematic unit. Post a large planning chart that gives categories for planning, such as the one below. Encourage your colleagues to use self-stick notes to add to "Resources" and "Learning Experiences." After sufficient time for input, meet to select and sequence ideas for the thematic unit. You may find that even teachers not directly involved in teaching the unit have resources and ideas to suggest.

## PLANNING CHART

| Theme: | Time Frame: |
|---|---|
| Content and Process Objectives: | Learning Experiences: |
| Resources: | Evaluation Measures: |

# Multicultural Infusion

## by Dr. Margaret A. Gallego

**Assistant Research Scientist, University of California, San Diego, Laboratory of Comparative Human Cognition**

> "Multicultural education involves changes in the total school or educational environment; it is not limited to curricular changes."
>
> James Banks
> Multicultural Education: Issues and Perspectives

A child is a member of several groups – a family, a classroom, a community, a culture. The interactions a child has had within these various groups since birth have helped create a unique individual. In a multicultural curriculum, the study of culture is incorporated into daily classroom activities, as much to honor each student's uniqueness as to learn about others. Since many basic outlooks and assumptions are formed in school, respect for diversity can and should be an underlying goal for every classroom.

## A Framework for Developing Cultural Awareness

The best way to understand others is to step into their shoes. For children, this means

- meaningful interactions with high-quality multicultural literature.
- becoming familiar with the contributions of all groups to American society.
- periods of immersion in various cultures.

Many teachers build units of study around related pieces of literature. Such a thematic unit might consist of

- an author study
- an illustrator study
- a group of stories, songs, and poems from a particular culture
- a topic from social studies, math, or science that connects to the stories, poems, plays, and informational texts students are reading
- investigation into the achievements and importance of one or more persons from a culture or group, highlighting how these achievements relate to topics and themes being studied.

One of the main purposes of a multicultural unit of study is to give all children opportunities to succeed, including children whose first language is not English. Building equity into the content is essential when planning a unit. The activities intended to reach this goal should enhance the reading, writing, speaking, and listening abilities of *every* child. For children acquiring English, teachers can support the first language by asking children to share stories, songs, sayings, and even recipes from home. Paying attention to children's first language shows respect for diversity. It also develops thinking skills and literary appreciation that transfer easily to English.

## Getting Started: Some Tips

Multicultural education takes a variety of forms. Some schools have opted for total immersion. Other schools have established separate learning centers that can accommodate small groups of students at a time. Some programs begin within a single classroom committed to cultural awareness, and then gradually spread awareness through the school. Whatever your situation, don't be afraid to take the plunge! Here are some tips for getting started:

✓ Help each child become aware of his or her heritage.

✓ Ask for help from family members and people in the community.

✓ Consider starting with the cultures represented by children in your classroom.

✓ Don't expect to immediately gather all the books, videos, and artifacts that you need to really bring a unit of study alive. Assume that each year you will acquire one or two outstanding new materials.

✓ Don't neglect to do some research of your own on the people your students will be studying.

✓ Don't be afraid to start with your own culture and heritage!

✓ Don't forget to read aloud regularly from literature that fairly represents the culture you are studying.

## Goals

Multicultural programs are nearly as diverse as the cultures they represent. However, some general goals pertain to all:

1. *Highlight the contributions* all *groups have made.* Find and share information about scientific, artistic, and other achievements by diverse members of society.

2. *Avoid stereotyping.* One way to do this is to be sure you represent every culture *as it is in the present,* as well as how it was in the past. All cultures are in a continual state of change.

3. *Put the literature to work for you.* A large part of your daily acitivities can be reading or listening to a story, song, or poem and then responding to it.

4. *Accentuate your students' languages, backgrounds, and cultures.* Exploring even the "outward trappings" of a culture—festivals, dances, costumes, artifacts, foods—can help students better understand and appreciate the attitudes and beliefs that define a particular culture.

5. *Avoid lumping groups of people together.* Focus on one group of people within a larger region, rather than trying to study a whole area as a single, definable entity. Much misinformation results when one tries to portray, for example, the whole Middle East, or all of Europe or of sub-Saharan Africa.

6. *Remember that multicultural ideas are "caught" rather than "taught."* The attitudes you are trying to develop in children cannot be taught in formal lessons. They come through everyday experiences in which respect for others is the rule.

# Achieving BALANCE in Our Literacy Programs

## by Dr. Dorothy S. Strickland
### The State of New Jersey Professor of Reading, Rutgers University

**New insights into learning and teaching have brought about numerous changes in literacy instruction in recent years, particularly in the early grades.**

Greater emphasis on writing and its relationship to reading, greater use of trade books, and increased attention to the integration of the language arts are among the most noticeable changes. Most would agree that there is much to celebrate. But, as with anything new, the changes have also brought about some confusion and frustration. A variety of factors may account for this.

- **At times, new ideas were embraced and implemented before they were clearly understood.**
- **At other times, change was only nominally accepted and more-familiar methods were imposed on the new curricular frameworks and materials.**
- **In still other cases, too many changes were imposed at once.**

As a result, many educators were made to feel as though they were struggling in a morass of change.

Today, in districts throughout the country, educators are once again reexamining the direction they have taken. They are wondering, "Have we gone too far in one direction or another? Have we abandoned some of the tried and true good practices of the past?" They want to know how they can take advantage of the best research and practice available today in a way that makes sense and is more effective for children, teachers, and parents. They are searching for balance.

When educators search for balance in their literacy programs, certain issues inevitably surface. Following is a list of some of these issues and suggestions for how they might be addressed.

### BALANCING A SKILLS EMPHASIS WITH A MEANING EMPHASIS

Neither skills nor meaning need ever be abandoned. Indeed, skills are learned best when taught through meaningful use. For example, after sharing a story that includes many examples of the same sound/letter relationship, such as /b/*b* or the inflectional ending *-ing*, point out the relationship and discuss it with children. Help them make a chart of other examples they find in their reading, and encourage them to use what they have learned in their own writing.

### BALANCING DIRECT AND INDIRECT INSTRUCTION

Direct instruction usually refers to the explicit transmission of knowledge. Indirect instruction involves providing opportunities for children to discover new ideas and strategies, to apply skills they have learned, and to assist one another as teachers and learners. Effective teaching will make use of both. For example, minilessons are key elements of contemporary literacy instruction. These are systematically planned, brief instructional episodes that focus on a single strategy for learning and that employ direct instructional methods. Minilessons make heavy use of the modeling and demonstration of skills. Teachers not only *tell;* they *show*. Showing how something is done is one of the most effective methods of direct instruction available. Still, that is not enough. For children to "own" a skill or strategy, they need opportunities to try it out on their own and to "discover" opportunities for its use. The most adept teachers are those who know how to provide a variety of opportunities for children to learn and to apply their learning in a meaningful way.

## BALANCING CONTENT AND PROCESS

Although the desire for information frequently inspires us to learn, learning involves much more than accumulating information. If we overemphasize content, children are left not knowing how to get information or to learn on their own. When teachers plan for instruction in science or social studies, for example, they need to keep both content and process goals in mind.

**Content goals** refer to the knowledge we hope children will gain from the topic under study, such as how plants grow or the kinds of helpers in the neighborhood. **Process goals** refer to what we hope children will be able to do at the end of the study—specifically, how to observe and chart the growth of a seedling over a period of time or how to interview a neighborhood helper and write a brief paragraph to share with the class. Process goals take children beyond the specific subject matter, helping them become skillful learners no matter what content is under study.

## BALANCING TRADE BOOKS AND TEXTBOOKS

In many school districts, textbooks continue to be the core materials in various curricular areas, providing a sense of continuity across grade levels. An effective literacy program embraces a wide variety of materials, including separately bound trade books. It may be helpful to think in terms of several layers of texts in the classroom. One layer might involve the literature selected by the teacher for real-aloud purposes. Another might be the core literacy program in which all children are involved, providing many opportunities for extension to trade books and

technology. Yet another layer might involve a variety of self-selected materials that children read independently. While these layers relate specifically to the literacy program, children should be involved with both core and trade book materials in every subject area. Each layer has an important role to play in a balanced program of instruction.

## BALANCING INFORMAL CLASSROOM ASSESSMENT AND NORM-REFERENCED STANDARDIZED TESTS

Shifting the balance away from standardized tests in favor of authentic classroom assessment methods is a goal that most educators applaud. Standardized tests are useful in rank-ordering pupils and, frequently, teachers and schools as well. However, they do little to help teachers focus on instructional needs. Schools are seeking to make greater use of performance-based assessment procedures, which are closely linked to the curriculum and also serve to inform the public about how well students are doing. For example, portfolios that include samples of a child's writing over time help both teacher and child get a sense of specific strengths and weaknesses. Probably most important, this type of ongoing assessment tends to make the criteria more clear to both child and teacher.

Achieving balance in our literacy programs should not imply that there is such a thing as "The Balanced Approach." Nor should it imply a sampling method in which a teacher selects a little of this and a little of that. Finally, it should not imply two very distinct, parallel approaches coexisting in a single classroom—for example, literature on Mondays and Wednesdays and skills the remainder of the week.

Ultimately, a teacher must make instructional decisions based on how children learn and how he or she can best teach them. More than likely this will never mean throwing out all of the methods used by any single teacher or school district. Needless to say, it will also not mean maintaining the status quo. Finding the balance takes knowledge, time, and thoughtfulness.

# Strategies Guide for Beginning Readers

## by Dr. W. Dorsey Hammond

**Even as competent educators, we sometimes need an additional strategy to use; or perhaps we need to be reminded of a workable strategy that we may have overlooked. Below are ten situations, each accompanied by teaching strategies that are usually successful in helping students learn.**

| Problem/Situation | Considerations | Suggested Instructional Strategies |
|---|---|---|
| **Has minimal knowledge of phonics.** | The issue is how to begin. Phonics and phonemic awareness are learned best while children are having extensive experiences with print. | • Begin with basic sounds in the environment such as clapping, snapping fingers, or tapping; and ask "Are these sounds the *same* or are they *different?*" <br> • Make sure students have concepts of *likeness* and *differences,* and *beginning, rhyming,* and *endings.* <br> • Deal with sounds in context of words. <br> • Use poetry, chants, songs, and so on, to focus on beginning sounds or rhyming sounds. <br> • Use predictable books, Big Books, and nursery rhymes. <br> • Model for students the tracking of print by moving your hand or finger along the print as you read aloud. |
| **Has difficulty recognizing words in isolation.** | Recognizing words in isolation is more difficult than recognizing words in context. | • Provide extensive opportunities to see and hear words. <br> • Encourage students to recognize individual words within context of story or sentence. For example, after reading a page, ask students to find and point to a certain word. <br> • Build a word bank or file of known words. |
| **Seems confused by phonics instruction.** | Some students find phonics overwhelming. | • Check students' understanding of concepts of *likeness, differences, beginning, ending,* and so on. <br> • Address sounds in the context of words. <br> • Chunk sounds as in *fast, last, past.* <br> • Say words *to* students or show the words boldly on the board or on a transparency. Have them say the words. <br> • Keep activities light and enjoyable. |
| **Tends to reverse letters and words.** | Reversals do not usually indicate a learning problem. Reversals tend to be a natural part of the early learning-to-read process. | • Continue with appropriate instruction in reading and writing. <br> • Put words in context. Students make less reversals when they have meaning to support their word recognition. <br> • Encourage students to look carefully at the beginning letters of words. <br> • Model for students the left-to-right process of reading words and sentences. <br> • Display the letters of the alphabet. |

| Problem/Situation | Considerations | Suggested Instructional Strategies |
|---|---|---|
| **Miscalls words when reading.** | This behavior often occurs with young readers. It is possible that students need to mature in their phonics ability. It is also possible that students need to pay more attention to the meaning, that is, what would make sense. | • Remind students to make sense of what they are reading.<br>• Refrain from correcting the reader until he or she has had time to self-correct.<br>• Intervene by asking the student to look carefully at the whole word. You might ask "What part do you already know?" or "Which part of the word is giving you trouble?" |
| **Seems to honor beginning sounds and then says *any* word with that particular sound, for example, *d*og for *d*one or *s*un for *s*and.** | When reading, students often feel pressured to produce a word very quickly by looking at the first letter and then guessing. | • Encourage students to make sense of what they are reading.<br>• Give students several words that have a common beginning and ask them to read the words with you, as in *friend*, *from*, *free*, and *fry*. These activities encourage young readers to look beyond the first letter.<br>• Sort words by endings. |
| **Has difficulty with ending sounds.** | This situation occurs with some emerging readers. | • Encourage reading in context where the sentence structure will help determine the appropriate ending.<br>• Identify a base word and show students how to change endings to produce a new word.<br>    Examples: *fast, faster, fastest*<br>• Encourage students to listen carefully to the endings of words. Use rhyming words, phonograms, and rhyming couplets. |
| **Has difficulty with vowel sounds.** | This is a common comment from classroom teachers and from parents.<br>    Vowels are highly unpredictable unless they are in context of other letters or letter combinations. As students mature in reading, their knowledge of vowel patterns will increase. | • Increase students' amount of reading.<br>• Encourage students to write and think about which letters represent particular sounds.<br>• Work with vowels in clusters or phonograms, such as f*a*st, l*a*st, p*a*st.<br>• Do word sorts. Encourage students to group or organize words by sound and letter patterns. |
| **Doesn't apply what he or she knows.** | Application needs to be taught as part of the process of learning phonics. | • Model for students the thinking process of what to do when they come to a word they don't know.<br>• Discuss the process, and make a chart:<br>  a. Think about what would make sense.<br>  b. Look at the beginning.<br>  c. Find the part of the word I already know.<br>  d. Think of another word that looks almost the same.<br>  e. Then ask for help. |
| **Has difficulty recognizing words quickly. Reads slowly word-by-word.** | Immediate recognition of words develops with maturity. There are many ways to enhance fluency and automaticity. | • Have students read familiar or predictable texts.<br>• Read *with* children in choral-reading situations. Read poetry and rhyme.<br>• Practice repeated readings—reading a segment of text several times until fluency is reached.<br>• Encourage students to combine groups of letters to produce sounds, as with phonograms, rhyming words, base words, and affixes.<br>• Encourage students to think about their reading. Reading for meaning increases word accuracy. |

# SHARED READING

## by Dr. Dorothy S. Strickland

**"Goodnight, Moon!" Three-year-old Ryan claps his hands and cuddles close to his mom as he yells out a line from one of his favorite books. His mother smiles and reads on, slowing her pace or remaining silent at key points where Ryan joins in "reading" aloud.**

For generations, shared reading experiences at home have helped countless youngsters approach beginning reading with joy and ease. In today's classrooms, teachers use this technique to extend the reading development of children who are lucky enough to have been read to at home and to provide a vital literacy experience for those who have not been read to.

## What is shared reading?

Shared reading is an interactive process in which teacher and children participate together to read a text. The text may be a big book, a chart, or any other print in the classroom environment. Predictable materials with repetitive pictures, words, and phrases work well. Shared reading can be used from prekindergarten right through the primary grades. The difficulty and complexity of the materials can be increased as children gain confidence and skill.

Repeated readings are key to the success of shared reading. Children need many varied experiences with familiar whole texts. Group discussion, art activities, shared writing, and drama are some of the different ways children might respond to the same text.

## Why is shared reading important?

- Students are provided with a model of a skilled, enthusiastic adult reader.

- Group reading is a positive, low-risk literacy experience.

- Instruction is automatically differentiated since all children can function at their own levels.

- Specific skills may be taught as children learn from and enjoy the text.

- Oral language is developed as children read with the group and participate in discussion.

# What happens during shared reading?

Shared reading involves a great deal of teacher/child interaction. Most importantly, both teacher and children are ACTIVE.

### Roles of Teacher and Child During Shared Reading

| Teacher | Child |
|---|---|
| Presents whole tasks | Experiences whole tasks |
| Performs with child | Performs with teacher |
| Gives active support | Gains knowledge |
| Intervenes when needed | Internalizes textual frameworks and language patterns |
| Gradually releases support | Internalizes strategies |
| Offers numerous and varied opportunities to apply what has been learned | Practices strategies, using whole texts in meaningful contexts |
| Introduces increasingly difficult tasks | |

# How will I know if children understood the story?

The first time you read a story, try to include the following:

1. A discussion of cover, title, and author
2. Opportunities for prediction
3. Follow-up activities:
   Confirm children's predictions.
   Help children relate the story to their personal experiences. Ask open-ended discussion questions:

   • What was your favorite part?
   • Has something like that ever happened to you?
   • What if _____ hadn't happened in the story?
   • How else could the story have ended?

# Why should I reread a story?

A story, poem, or song that is suitable for a shared reading should probably be reread several times, unless, of course, your children did not like it. If the story was first read purely for enjoyment, a lot of learning opportunities are lost if the story is not read at least one more time. Here's just a short list:

1. Increasing participation
2. Exploring conventions of print
3. Extending comprehension
4. Expanding vocabulary
5. Responding creatively; relating to other curriculum areas

## Increasing Participation

a. **Choral reading**   With each rereading, more and more children are able to join in and recite more and more of the text, with ever greater accuracy. Repeated readings of a classic like Brown Bear, *Brown Bear, What Do You See?* will illustrate this perfectly. With each rereading, children are attending to picture clues (red bird, purple cat), clues from repetitions built into the text (*what do you see?/looking at me*), and clues from their own understanding of the story. (Animals take turns telling what they see.)

b. **Other ways to join in**   Depending on the story, children can create sound effects, make hand/body movements, or clap to the rhythm of the story line. The text patterns of some stories lend themselves to special group configurations. For example, when rereading *Brown Bear,* a teacher might have half the class ask the questions and the other half recite the answers.

**c. Questions and discussion** The very first time they hear a story, children want and deserve an uninterrupted reading. The second or third time through, however, there's time to really pick apart the story and to explore elements that intrigue or confuse individual children. During subsequent readings, you and your class can

- ask or answer questions that arise during the reading.
- talk in depth about the pictures.
- let individuals share similar experiences they've had.
- discuss vocabulary.

## Exploring Conventions of Print

**a. Book awareness** For very inexperienced readers, this may be as fundamental as identifying the basic parts of a book and what they are for. It also means knowing where to start reading—in the book and on each page.

**b. Words, spaces, letters, punctuation** Big books and charts are wonderful tools for minilessons about:

- *words and word spaces* Frame words with your hands, and talk about how they're separated; have children do the same. Have children count how many times a particular word is repeated on a page or in an entire story. Have children find all the words with the same beginning or ending letters or sounds, all the words that start with the same sound as their first name, and all the words that begin with a capital letter. With a self-stick note, cover a word that you think children will be able to predict. Ask the group to guess the word as you read the page aloud together.

- *letters* Frame a word, and talk about the letters in it. How many are there? How many of any single letter? Whose name begins with one of the letters?

Which letter or letters stand for the beginning sound you hear when you say the word? Is this *g* written the same way that you write a *g*? How are the *g*'s different?

- *sentences, capitalization, and punctuation* Make phrase and sentence strips for children to find and match with repeated test in the big book. Children can practice reading the words within the story first and then on the sentence strip. Have volunteers find the capital letter that begins each sentence, and talk about this rule. Point out that the word *I* is always written as a capital letter. Talk about different end marks and why they are used with statements, commands, questions, and exclamations.

## Extending Comprehension

**a. Predicting** Even after young children have heard a story several times, they still love to predict what will happen next. You can make this more challenging by asking them to identify picture clues they use, clues from their own experiences, or clues from the structure of the story itself.

**b. Sequencing** Have volunteers help you make sequencing cards based on events in the story. A story like *Flower Garden* is easy for children to sequence because the events take place in a logical order. Let a group of children work together to hold up the cards in sequence during one shared reading of the story.

**c. Finding patterns** Have children express in their own words the pattern in a predictable story. Children can also discuss similarities and differences among stories they know: "How is 'Five Little Ducks' like the song 'Roll Over'?" (One is subtracted each time.)

**d. Classifying/Categorizing**  Have children make lists of people, places, animals, and things that arise naturally from the story. For example, they might make lists of large and small animals; fierce and friendly animals; and one-legged, two-legged, four-legged, and six-legged animals after reading *Who Is the Beast?* Post the lists where children can add to them and use them in their own writing.

## Expanding Vocabulary

**a. Synonyms**  With a self-stick note, cover a word that children are likely to know within the context of the story, such as *littlest* or *biggest* in "The Three Billy-Goats Gruff." Ask children to supply other words that mean about the same thing. Write them on the note, and reread that part of the story, using the children's words.

**b. Imagery**  Children can substitute other animals in a story like *Quick as a Cricket.* (quick as a deer; mean as a bee) Make new big books using their ideas and illustrations.

**c. Word webs**  Put on the board an important story word such as friend from *My Friends* or *peanut butter* from the jingle "Peanut Butter and Jelly." Have children brainstorm associated words to add to the web. Display the web where children can add to it and can use the words in their writing.

## What can I learn from a shared reading?

Most often, shared reading in the class-room is a group experience. It is an excellent opportunity to *observe* the overall progress of the group. Later, when you *analyze* the information from your obser-vations, you have a basis for planning future learning experiences.

During shared readings, you can also focus on the development of specific individuals. An individual might be selected for special monitoring because of one of the following reasons:

**1.** The child rarely participates in the group. Could he or she have a visual or an auditory problem? Is the problem shyness or limited language development?Is there a distraction that prevents this child from fully participating?

**2.** The child appears to be functioning at a very advanced level. Could he or she handle more challenging materials? Would this child feel comfortable being a buddy reader with a less able classmate?

Use the copying master on the next page to help you assess the progress of your group during shared readings throughout the year.

# Shared Reading Observational Checklist

Child _____ Teacher _____ Grade _____

| Concepts About Print<br>*Child demonstrates understanding of the following concepts:* | Date | Date | Date | Date | Date | Date |
|---|---|---|---|---|---|---|
| Print contains meaning | | | | | | |
| Pictures convey and enhance meaning | | | | | | |
| Left-to-right direction | | | | | | |
| Top-to-bottom direction | | | | | | |
| Book title | | | | | | |
| Author | | | | | | |
| Illustrator | | | | | | |
| Sentence | | | | | | |
| Word | | | | | | |
| Letter | | | | | | |
| Similarities in words and letters | | | | | | |

| Comprehension and Interpretation<br>*Child demonstrates understanding of familiar books and stories through the following behaviors:* | Date | Date | Date | Date | Date | Date |
|---|---|---|---|---|---|---|
| Discusses meanings related to characters and events | | | | | | |
| Makes and confirms reasonable predictions | | | | | | |
| Infers words in cloze-type activities | | | | | | |
| Remembers sequence of events | | | | | | |
| Compares/contrasts events within and between books | | | | | | |
| States main ideas | | | | | | |
| States causes and effects | | | | | | |
| Recalls details | | | | | | |

| Interest in Books and Reading<br>*Child demonstrates an interest in books and reading through the following behaviors:* | Date | Date | Date | Date | Date | Date |
|---|---|---|---|---|---|---|
| Shows interest in listening to stories | | | | | | |
| Participates in reading patterned and predictable language | | | | | | |
| Engages in talk about books and stories | | | | | | |
| Requests favorite books to be read aloud | | | | | | |
| Views himself/herself as a reader | | | | | | |
| Voluntarily uses the classroom library | | | | | | |
| Shows pleasure in reading independently | | | | | | |

# Practice Might Make Perfect, but Rehearsal Makes for Fluency and Fun

■ BY DR. NANCY ROSER ■

In some of the earliest preprimers designed for beginning readers, a carefully chosen set of words was introduced at a prescribed rate and systematically repeated. Arthur Gates (1930) had shown that children of average intelligence needed about 35 repetitions of words just in their school materials to "give reading ability a healthy birth and capacity to live and grow" (p. 35). As a result, learning to read (in school, at least) meant learning a defined set of words that, when combined, resulted in stories with stilted syntax and simple plots. Yet, the repetition of words ensured exposure and practice. Children (like me) read:

> ## "Run, run, run."
> ## and
> ## "Funny, funny Sally."

We read our preprimer stories over and over until our reading sounded smooth and fluent. It was much like learning to play the piano in those days. Because our piano teachers expected fluent (smooth and accurate) performance, we played the same scales repeatedly until we got them right—five times saying the notes, five times singing them, five times counting—over and over and over. [Who knows whether so many of us are piano drop-outs because our practice made us "perfect" players of scales, but not of pianos.] And, just as we repeatedly practiced our scales, so did we read those little stories again and again—out loud, silently, in turns, and chorally—not at all certain that we were becoming "readers."

No one doubts that beginners must read to get good at it, yet our ideas of what constitutes the best practice opportunities for beginners have changed (just as, no doubt, the ideas of piano teachers have changed). To get practice with text today, children are not only grounded in the alphabetic system of written language (sounds and the letters that record them), but are also presented with a host of manageable texts—"little books"—to read. These "learning to read" materials have plot lines and characters, are often written by noteworthy authors, vary in genre, and are arrayed in baby-step increments of difficulty, so that children can be both interested and successful *en route* to becoming readers. Still, not every beginning reader, even those fortunate enough to have hosts of little books and much opportunity to read, become "fluent." Their reading isn't as smooth and accurate and expressive as their peers. Instead, it may be characterized as "word-by-word," marked by long pauses, frequent repetitions, poor intonation, and errors. In that important period in which many children are beginning to "become unglued" from the print (Chall,1983), some simply don't.

Second graders are ideal candidates for fluency practice because they have had instruction in the written code, and are eager to "show what they know" about reading. To help children achieve fluency, teachers have used a variety of approaches, including demonstrations by proficient readers, repeated readings of the same story, and extensive reading at an independent level. My colleagues and I (Miriam Martinez and Susan Strecker) have been working with second graders to help them become more fluent readers by turning their reading practice into "rehearsals," their stories into "scripts," and their reading groups into "repertory companies." We worked like this: First, we found examples of good stories that lent themselves well to readers' theatre scripts. We used the attributes of readers' theatre to define our task because we wanted readers to practice (reread)—but to do so purposefully and in ways that were fun.

## Getting Started

To get started, you simply make a copy of the script for each child, highlighting all of a character's lines on each script. When a child is passed a script, he or she knows exactly what part to read while holding that particular copy.

Next, each child is assigned to a repertory group that "fits" or matches the children's instructional level. There should be comfort but also room to improve. Accuracy, rate, phrasing, and expressiveness are all affected when the text is too difficult.

**Readers' theatre** *is essentially theatre without props, costumes, or stage movements. Rather than memorizing parts, readers read from scripts, sometimes sitting on stools or standing before the audience. A narrator makes certain that the audience has the full sense of the drama by supplying the descriptive or narrative parts of the story. The readers bring the characters to life, making images and actions vivid through the interpretive power of their voices. That makes rehearsal necessary. And, deep comprehension is required so the nuances of character can be made evident with only voice (and facial expression) as substitutes for full staging. A story that makes a good script is within the readers' reach, has dialogue, enough roles for several children, and a plot line that can be carried by the narrator's voice.*

**We use a five-day sequence for teaching and rehearsal that works like this:**

Children are introduced to and read the original story. The children participate in a literature discussion. The teacher conducts a mini-lesson on some aspect of fluency (such as what punctuation marks help readers understand, or how the author's words help readers know what characters are feeling). Children may read the story again by themselves or with a friend.

Copies of the scripts are distributed. Children read a highlighted part. They pass the scripts and read a new part. If there are more children in the group than parts, roles switch about half way through.

Children rehearse again, passing scripts and changing roles as they did on Day 2. During the last five minutes, children decide their roles for Friday's performance. (This takes negotiation and, at the beginning, is often the least smooth part of the sequence.)

Children spend the session practicing their final role in preparation for the next day's production. In the last few minutes, they may make character labels and decide where each will stand during the performance.

Repertory groups "perform" their readers' theatre for others—either other repertory groups, class guests, or younger children.

---

[1] If you have more than one group participating in readers theatre, you may choose to start each group on a different day

## What We Found Happens in Readers' Theatre

■ Readers *read* in readers' theatre. Typical stories (like scales) lose their enticement with so many replays, but not in readers' theatre. Changing parts, and rehearsing to get characters right are enough to keep interest high. Readers read the stories an average of 15–20 times (as opposed to the one or two times) many stories are reread.

■ Readers read better using readers' theatre scripts. The children we work with read faster, more accurately, and smoother with the materials they practice (Dahl & Samuels, 1984; Dowhower, 1987, 1989.) But that seems obvious, doesn't it? Yet, there's an even more hopeful indicator: These children read other materials more fluently, too. That is, rates and accuracy increase on materials they have not yet rehearsed, indicating that the "practice" effect transfers, much as the piano teacher hoped my endless scales would transfer to the Moonlight Sonata.

■ Finally, young readers like readers' theatre. They tell us they like to practice in groups, like to prepare for performances, and love the genuinely delighted audience reaction.

## An Example of Readers' Theatre

The following script was based on "Hedgehog Bakes a Cake" in ***Something New (Collections,*** Level 2-1). You can compare this version with the original to see how very minor the changes are between this script and the original story. Changes are made only to clarify a pronoun referent or to make something depicted in the illustration clearer. In some instances, the narrator's lines can be shortened to help make for an interesting performance.

### What to Look For

*Fluent 7-year-olds may read at a rate of 70 to 90 words per minute. Take a rate and accuracy "reading" of selected children at the beginning and end of the week to see how the practice affects your children's fluency.*

### References

Chall, J. (1983). *Stages of Reading Development.* New York: McGraw-Hill.

Dahl, P. R. & Samuels, S. J. (1974). A mastery based experimental program for teaching poor readers high speed word recognition skills. Unpublished manuscript, University of Minnesota, Minneapolis.

Dowhower, S. L. (1987). Effect of repeated reading on second grade transitional readers' fluency and comprehension. *Reading Research Quarterly, 22,* 389–406.

Dowhower, S. L. (1989). Repeated reading: Research into practice. *The Reading Teacher, 42,* 502–507.

Gates, A. I. (1930). *Interest and Ability in Reading.* New York: Macmillan.

Martinez, M.; Roser, N.; & Strecker, S. (1999). "I never thought I could be a star": A Readers Theatre ticket to fluency. *The Reading Teacher, 52,* 326–334.

© Harcourt

# Hedgehog Bakes a Cake

**Characters:**
    Narrators I and II
      *(role divided to make more parts)*
    Hedgehog
    Rabbit
    Squirrel
    Owl

**Narrator:**

We are performing a Readers' Theatre of *Hedgehog Bakes a Cake* by Maryann Macdonald. You'll find our story in **Something New** on page 199.

The part of Hedgehog is played by _____. (or, if Hedgehog's part is divided between two actor/readers, both can be introduced)

The part of Rabbit is played by _____.

The part of Squirrel is played by _____.

The part of Owl is played by _____.

The part of the first narrator is played by me, _____.

The part of the second narrator is played by _____.

And now, *Hedgehog Bakes a Cake*....

**Narrator:**     *Hedgehog was hungry for cake. He found a yellow cake recipe.*

**Hedgehog:**     This one sounds easy…and good, too.

**Narrator:**     *Hedgehog took out the flour, the eggs, and the butter. He was taking out the blue mixing bowl when he heard a knock at the door.*

**Rabbit:**     Knock knock.

**Narrator:**     *It was Rabbit.*

**Hedgehog:**     Hello, Rabbit. I am making a cake.

**Rabbit:**     I will help you. I am good at making cakes.

**Hedgehog:**     Here is the recipe.

**Rabbit:**     You do not need this recipe. I will show you what to do.

**Narrator:**     *Rabbit took the flour. He dumped it into the blue bowl. He took the butter and dumped that in, too. Then he dumped in the sugar.*

**Rabbit:**     Now we will mix it.

**Narrator:**     *Mixing was hard work. Rabbit mixed and mixed. His arm began to hurt. The batter was lumpy. The sugar stuck to the sides of the bowl. There was flour everywhere.*

**Rabbit:**     I think someone is calling me. You finish the mixing, Hedgehog. I will come back when the cake is ready.

**Narrator:**     *Hedgehog shook his head. The cake batter was a mess.*

**Squirrel:**     What's the matter, Hedgehog?

| | |
|---|---|
| **Narrator:** | *Squirrel was at the door, looking in.* |
| **Hedgehog:** | I am making a cake. But it doesn't look very good. |
| **Squirrel:** | You need eggs. I will put them in. |
| **Narrator:** | *Squirrel cracked some eggs and dropped them in. Some egg shell fell in, too.* |
| **Squirrel:** | A little bit of shell does not matter. Mix it all together. |
| **Narrator:** | *So Hedgehog mixed. The batter was more lumpy, but mixing was easier than before. Owl stuck her head in the door.* |
| **Owl:** | Baking? May I help? |
| **Narrator:** | *Hedgehog did not want more help. But he didn't want to hurt Owl's feelings.* |
| **Hedgehog:** | You can butter the pan. |
| **Owl:** | I'll just dip my wing into this butter and smear it around the pan. |
| **Narrator:** | *Owl turned on the oven with her buttery feathers. She turned it up as high as it would go.* |
| **Owl:** | The oven must be nice and hot. |
| **Squirrel:** | We have gotten very messy helping you. We will go home now and clean up. Put the cake in the oven. We will come back when it is ready. |
| **Narrator:** | *Squirrel and Owl went home. Hedgehog looked at the kitchen. There was sugar on the floor. There was butter on the oven door. And there was flour on everything.* |
| **Hedgehog:** | I better dump this cake batter into the garbage pail. |
| **Narrator:** | *Hedgehog locked the kitchen door and took out his recipe. First, Hedgehog measured the sugar. He mixed it slowly with the butter. Next he counted out three eggs and cracked them into the bowl.* |
| **Hedgehog:** | One, two, three. |
| **Narrator:** | *Then he added the flour. Hedgehog mixed everything together and poured it into Owl's buttery pan. He turned down the heat and put the batter in the oven. Then he cleaned the kitchen.* |
| **Owl, Squirrel, Rabbit:** | Knock, knock, knock. |
| **Rabbit:** | Open the door, Hedgehog. We can smell the cake, and we are getting hungry. |
| **Narrator:** | *Hedgehog unlocked the door. The kitchen was clean. The cake was cooling on a rack. And the table was set for a tea party. The four friends sat down. Hedgehog cut the cake. They each ate one slice. Then they each ate another slice.* |
| **Rabbit:** | This is the best cake I have ever made. Aren't you glad I showed you how to do it? |
| **Squirrel:** | The eggs made it very rich. And you can't taste the shell at all. |
| **Owl:** | It's perfect. I set the oven just right. |
| **Hedgehog:** | Thank you all for your help. Next time I will try to do it all by myself. |
| **Narrator:** | *Thank you for your attention. Please stay after because we want you to have a taste of Hedgehog's Yellow Cake!* |

# Learning Styles and Multiple Intelligences

## WHAT THEY ARE AND WHAT TO DO ABOUT THEM

*by Dr. Guy Blackburn, Policy Analyst Consultant,*
*Oakland Schools, Waterford, Michigan*

Teachers already know that children learn at different rates and in different ways. Skillful, experienced teachers adapt their teaching techniques and learning activities to respond to these apparent differences. In recent years, learning theorists have provided teachers with new insights into how students learn and how to effectively organize instruction for students who seem to fit certain patterns of learning.

Two such approaches are the theory of "learning styles, or learning modalities," as presented in the work of Rita Dunn and Bernice McCarthy, and the theory of "multiple intelligences," as presented by Howard Gardner. What these theories have in common is that they focus on what occurs in the minds of learners as they undertake a task or attempt to learn something. This article provides suggestions and formats for practical applications of each theory.

By glancing forward to the Classroom Activities chart, you will see some practical examples for addressing different learning modalities and intelligences. Take a look at page 58 now, and then return and read the rest of this brief description of the theories behind the activities.

This will allow you to tie practice to theory immediately.

Now let's take a look at each theory and its general applications to the classroom.

### Learning Styles or Modalities

For years, Rita Dunn has encouraged teachers to alter instruction to meet the learning styles of children. She has also pointed out that teachers have preferred styles, and that the happiest situation is when the teacher's style and the child's style match. Such a match is probably impossible when there are twenty-five to thirty children in a classroom. So it is imperative, according to Dunn, that teachers systematically screen children and adjust teaching and learning experiences to their learning styles. (The phrase *learning modalities* sometimes replaces the term *learning styles.*) The major modes, or styles, are these:

 **VISUAL:** These learners learn more easily when they *see* things.

 **AUDITORY:** These learners acquire knowledge more readily through *listening*.

 **VERBAL:** Verbal learners prefer to learn through talking and expressing their thoughts in writing.

 **TACTILE/KINESTHETIC:** This modality allows for children who tend to learn best from touching things and manipulating concrete objects.

 **SMELL AND TASTE:** Although these modalities of learning are restricted by practical considerations, it must be acknowledged that some learners use these senses to learn or to augment learning.

Think of children with whom you have worked, and try to identify those who rely heavily on one of these modes to learn. Next, think of yourself, and see whether you can identify the mode that best defines the way you learn. Now, think in general terms about what you can do to be sure that students are given opportunities to use their preferred mode. You may want to look again at the list of examples provided on page 60. Use these as springboards to come up with your own ideas to help children read, enjoy literature, and write.

## Left Brain/Right Brain: The Hemisphericity Theory

Another popular theory that speaks to learning styles is the hemisphericity theory, which refers to "right" and "left" brain functions. Bernice McCarthy, drawing on popular interpretations of brain research, has established another framework for teaching and learning, called the 4mat System. The basis of the system is the idea that the left hemisphere of the brain controls such functions as mathematics, sequencing, and logic, while the right hemisphere operates in areas such as visual imagery, spatial understanding, and intuition.

The assertion of McCarthy and others is that schools have traditionally overemphasized left brain development and ignored right brain functions. This can be seen in how curriculum and instruction typically rely on logical ordering in reading, writing, and math. McCarthy's theory encourages teachers to provide a variety of activities so that children can experience learning with both sides of the brain.

Take a look again at the list of activities on page 58, and see whether you can figure out which side of the brain each activity would stimulate or utilize.

## Howard Gardner's Theory of Multiple Intelligences

For most of this century, human intelligence has been measured by aptitude tests or I.Q. tests, in which a child is assigned a single number as a measure of her or his intelligence. These tests typically measure verbal and math abilities that relate directly to what children traditionally do in school. Two major problems have emerged with I.Q. scores. First, they have traditionally been viewed as stable and permanent measures of a child's intelligence. This has often led to limiting expectations for future learning. Second, this approach to intelligence ignores any other talents that a child might have.

Gardner has come up with eight clusters of intelligence that he believes provide a better model of human intelligence. He asserts that education should systematically provide for all of these clusters, instead of relying solely on the traditional modes of learning. Gardner further asserts that his model represents eight "intelligences," and he has developed scales and measures to identify them. Gardner's eight intelligences are:

1. **VERBAL/LINGUISTICS:** The ability to think in words and to use language to acquire, process, and express complex meaning.

2. **LOGICAL/MATHEMATICAL:** The ability to calculate, quantify, consider propositions and hypotheses, and carry out complex mathematical operations.

3. **SPATIAL/VISUAL:** The ability to think and express oneself in three dimensions such as in art or architecture.

4. **BODILY/KINESTHETIC:** The development of highly refined physical skills, as demonstrated by dancers, athletes, and crafts workers.

5. **MUSICAL/RHYTHMIC:** The ability to think in music, to hear, recognize, remember and manipulate patterns.

6. **INTERPERSONAL:** The capacity to work and communicate effectively with other people; effective teachers, counselors, and politicians tend to exhibit a high level of this intelligence.

7. **INTRAPERSONAL:** The ability to clearly know oneself and to perceive and develop an accurate and effective internal model for self-direction.

8. **NATURALIST:** The ability to discriminate among living things; having a sensitivity to features of our natural world.

Obviously, many children and adults have strengths in more than one of these "intelligences," but when individuals develop one area they can become highly skilled in fields such as art, athletics, politics, or music. Children who show promise in any of these areas should be viewed as intelligent, regardless of their performance on academic tests of math and verbal ability. Gardner further asserts that teachers specifically and schools generally should provide activities and programs that encourage the development of intelligences other than traditional verbal and mathematical abilities.

Take another look at the list of eight intelligences. This time, do a self-check first. Ask yourself which of Gardner's categories best fits you. Next, see whether there is an intelligence on the list that you naturally have but that is underdeveloped. Write yourself a message about how you feel about this underdevelopment, and ask yourself what you might do about exploring the neglected area. Doing this can help you think about the types, variety, and quality of activities that you provide for your students. Now look again at the classroom activities on page 60, and see whether you can identify some that would help students develop one or more of Gardner's intelligences.

No one knows what actually happens in the minds of learners as they receive and process new information and turn it into useful knowledge. However, by considering the theories and practices presented here, you can increase the likelihood that more children will learn effectively. We encourage you to weigh the theories according to your own experiences in learning and teaching important information and skills.

# CLASSROOM ACTIVITIES

As you read these examples, try to identify the learning style and the type of intelligence each is intended to foster. Also consider which side of the brain is tapped by each activity.

| | Learning Style | Type of Intelligence | Side of the Brain |
|---|---|---|---|
| **1.** Ask students to write a description of the person they most admire and include the reasons they chose this person. | _____ | _____ | _____ |
| **2.** Ask students to draw, paint, or assemble a collage to depict a story or a major event in a story. Have each child describe her or his representation to a group. | _____ | _____ | _____ |
| **3.** Ask students to identify a popular song that would go with a favorite story and then create an accompanying dance that expresses the story characters' emotions. | _____ | _____ | _____ |
| **4.** Have students use a story map or some other graphic organizer to represent the important elements of a story. | _____ | _____ | _____ |
| **5.** Soak strips of paper in perfume, aftershave, lemon juice, and vinegar. Have each student write words to describe the scent. Encourage students to compare their words. | _____ | _____ | _____ |
| **6.** Encourage students to write a poem about their favorite foods. As a prewriting activity, have them brainstorm a web of describing words for each food. | _____ | _____ | _____ |

Design and label two of your own activities.

**7.** _____

_____

_____     _____   _____   _____

**8.** _____

_____

_____     _____   _____   _____

| KEY | | |
|---|---|---|
| **Learning Style** | **Type of Intelligence** | **Side of the Brain** |
| **1.** Verbal | 1, 6 | Left |
| **2.** Visual, Tactile/Kinesthetic, Verbal | 1, 4, 7 | Right |
| **3.** Auditory, Tactile/Kinesthetic | 2, 5, 6 | Right |
| **4.** Visual, Verbal | 1, 3, 4 | Right |
| **5.** Verbal, Smell | 1, 7 | Right/Left |
| **6.** Verbal, Taste | 1, 4 | Right/Left |

© Harcourt

# Capitalizing on Students' Reading Styles

## by Dr. Marie Carbo

Founder and Executive Director of the National Reading Styles Institute
Syosset, New York

### Reading Style = Learning Style for Reading

Place two children of equal intelligence and similar backgrounds in the same reading program. One easily learns to read. The other struggles. Why? One possibility is differences in reading styles. A person's reading style is his or her learning style during the act of reading. Our individual reading style predisposes us to learn easily by means of certain reading techniques but not others. Students' reading styles can be identified with the *Reading Style Inventory*® (RSI), which also recommends compatible reading strategies, methods, and materials.

## Reading Styles of Low Achievers

Low achievers tend to be

- tactile (hands-on learners).
- kinesthetic (learn through whole-body movement).
- global (emotional, intuitive).
- group-oriented (energized by working in groups).
- mobile (need to move as they learn).

## Accommodating Reading Styles of Low Achievers

- Use hands-on activities instead of worksheets.
- Use kinesthetic strategies to teach skills (floor games, pantomiming, role-playing).
- Model a passage *before* children read it in pairs or alone—that is, shared reading, recorded books, choral reading.
- Deemphasize phonics if students are not auditory.
- Provide the option of working in pairs or small groups on reading activities.
- Provide breaks for snacks and movement; have comfortable reading areas available.
- Rehearse management procedures; for example, have children practice correct behaviors by pantomiming or role-playing.

## How to Record Books for High Reading Gains

Low-level readers are often bored by low-level reading materials. You can provide these students with challenging books that will motivate them and raise their reading abilities. How? Simply by recording challenging books in a special way so that the spoken and written words are synchronized for your students. These recordings provide students with plenty of practice before they read on their own. By providing a model of what good reading sounds like, this method of recording books increases children's reading fluency and improves their speech patterns and writing.

## CAPITALIZING ON READING STYLES

©1995 Marie Carbo

| READING STYLE | STRENGTHS/TENDENCIES | LEARN TO READ BEST |
|---|---|---|
| VISUAL | • Recall what they see<br>• Learn by observing | With "sight" methods, graphics, stories on filmstrips or videos |
| AUDITORY | • Recall what they hear<br>• Learn by listening | With phonics, choral reading, recordings, discussing stories |
| TACTILE | • Recall what they touch<br>• Learn by touching | With writing/tracing methods, language experience, games |
| KINESTHETIC | • Recall what they experience<br>• Learn through experience | By pantomiming, acting, floor games |
| GLOBAL | • Emotional, intuitive, spontaneous, random, inventive | With holistic methods (recorded books, story writing, projects) |
| ANALYTIC | • Logical planners, organizers, detail-oriented | With phonics (if they are auditory), programmed materials |

## Formula for Success

If the gap between the student's reading level and the level of the book is small, record about five to fifteen minutes of a story on one tape side at fairly normal pace, with natural expression and phrasing. If the gap is large, use a slower pace, fewer words to a phrase, exaggerate your expression somewhat, and record much less—only about two to three minutes.

## Creating Your Recordings

### Use a Slightly Slow Recording Pace

Record small amounts of high-interest reading material, using a slightly slow reading pace, good expression, and short, natural phrases. By "slightly slow," I mean slow enough so that the student can visually track the words but not so slow that interest begins to wane. Record as if you were actually reading to a child, with good expression. Just slow down a bit.

### Record a Small Amount on Each Tape Side

Place a small amount of text on each tape side—as little as two minutes. Low-performing readers can listen to the recording while they follow along in the book, without becoming bored or overwhelmed. After two or three listenings, most students are able to read the passage fluently. (Note: Even short books will require four to ten tape sides.)

### Use Short, Natural Phrases

Record passages in short, natural phrases so that the printed page is translated into meaningful segments. The slight pauses between phrases help to increase word recognition because they provide time for the listener's brain to absorb the printed material. Pause slightly longer than usual at commas and periods, too.

### Choose Books to Record

Books for this recorded-book method should be above the student's reading level. Use the chart below to guide your book selection. First, find the student's reading level and grade level. Next, locate the box where these two levels intersect. Begin the student with a recorded book on that reading level. For students with low language proficiency, you may need to start with lower-level books.

Example: For a student with a reading level of grade 3 and a grade level of 5, begin with a recorded book on the reading level of grade 4.

### Equipment and Materials

- One high-quality tape recorder and microphone for recording
- Tape players and headsets for individual students
- A listening center with headsets for groups
- Blank audiocassettes (seven to ten minutes per side; light colors for easy labeling)

| Student's Reading Level | Student's Grade Level | | | |
|---|---|---|---|---|
| | 3 | 4 | 5 | 6 |
| Preprimer | PP–1 | PP–1 | PP–1 | PP–1 |
| Primer | 1 | 1 | 1 | 1 |
| Grade 1 | 1–2 | 1–2 | 1–3 | 1–3 |
| Grade 2 | 2–3 | 3 | 3–4 | 3–4 |
| Grade 3 | 3–4 | 4 | 4–5 | 4–5 |
| Grade 4 | 4–6 | 4–6 | 5–6 | 5–7 |
| Grade 5 | 5–6 | 5–6 | 6–7 | 6–8 |

# STUDENTS WITH SPECIAL NEEDS:
## SOME SUGGESTIONS FOR READING SUCCESS

by Edna Cucksey-Stephens

With increasing coordination between regular and special education services, many learners with special needs are being mainstreamed into regular classroom reading programs. The expectation is that learning disabled students will be "fully included" rather than just "mainstreamed." This has caused concern for many teachers. "How will I ever meet the needs of these students in my classroom?" they ask.

The first step in meeting the needs of these students is to view them as capable learners. Though the reading difficulties of learning disabled students may be severe, effective reading instruction for them is in many ways no different from effective meaning-based, holistic instruction for other students. This article offers ideas and strategies that can be used to fully include learning disabled students in a classroom that promotes excellence for all students.

## Foster close collaboration between special education and general education teachers.
- Equally share the responsibility for the student's success.
- Work together to develop a plan for success that builds on the student's strengths.
- Establish goals and expectations for each student. Discuss these goals and expectations with the student.
- Schedule regular meetings to plan lessons and monitor the student's progress.
- Engage in team teaching when possible.

## Foster close collaboration between school and home.
- Send home regular progress reports that focus on the positive.
- Explain the reading program and helpful reading strategies at a parent meeting or through a newsletter.
- Encourage parents to read to or with their children daily.
  — If the child's home language is not English, family members should be encouraged to read aloud in the home language.

## Teach vocabulary and skills in meaningful contexts.
- Learning disabled students often have difficulty applying skills taught in isolation.
  — Providing concrete examples whenever possible will help students retain new words and concepts.
- Encourage each student to talk or write about his or her interests. Record the student's language, or have the student speak into a tape recorder and use the recording as a basis for writing. The written product can be used to teach vocabulary or other skills in a meaningful context.
- A student's retelling of a story that has been read aloud by the teacher or a peer can be used similarly. This is a good way to monitor students' comprehension skills.

## Teach and model effective reading strategies.

- Talk about what a strategy is and why it is important.
  - Explain that good readers have a purpose for reading.
  - Tell students that good readers look at pictures and graphics for clues.
  - Encourage students to build on what they know.
  - Most importantly, point out that good readers always try to make sense.
- Ask often, "What strategies can you use when you come to a word that you do not know?" Encourage students to read an unknown word as a blank and finish the sentence, and then to come back to see what word would make sense.
  - Also encourage students to ask you or another student for help when context, phonics, and structural analysis are not enough.
- Have students use a bookmark, word cards, or a word log to keep a running list of new and interesting words.
- Help students become aware of the strategies they already use. Encourage them to write about these strategies in a daily journal.

## Read aloud to students every day.

- You may wish to tape some of the stories you read. These can be used by students at another time.
  - Students can retell the important parts of the story after listening.
- Before a story is read to the whole class,
  - students can listen to the story on tape and follow along.
  - students can read it with a peer or have the peer read it aloud.

- access students' prior knowledge.
- encourage students to set purposes for reading by using prediction strategies.

## Use more graphic and visual aids, and depend less on verbal communication.

- Visually model strategies and skills to the entire class. For example, the special education teacher might fill in a semantic web or take notes on the overhead projector while the general education teacher is reading on informational article.
  - The teacher using the graphic should pause occasionally to "think aloud" about the process.

## Ask important questions that encourage students to analyze and interpret, not just recall fact.

- Encourage students to tell how a story relates to their own lives.
- Begin a dialogue journal with students. (See pages 18–19.)

## Encourage students to take risks without fear of "failure."

- Help all class members understand that different people are talented in different ways and that they must support each other's efforts to grow in new areas.
- Explain that making mistakes is part of the learning process; "no pain, no gain."
- Provide positive feedback when students make efforts to extend their reach.

# Reading Success for All Children

by Edna Cucksey-Stephens

Low-achieving children present us with some of our most challenging teaching. They can also provide some of our most rewarding experiences. The belief that all children can become successful readers is the key to our teaching and their learning. Low achievers often need more of our time and patience, but they benefit from the same meaning-based, holistic instruction as other children.

These reluctant readers often see themselves as "not very good" at reading. They may have poor self-esteem and sometimes feel "stupid" when their reading is not successful. The following ideas and suggestions will empower these children to be more self-confident about their reading ability and thus improve their reading success.

## Conference individually with low-achieving children.

- Communicate your belief that they can succeed.
- Explain that you will be a partner in their learning.
- Discuss reading as an interactive process in which the reader is just as important as the text.
- Stress meaning and "making sense."
- Accept children's personal responses to texts.
- Talk about children's interests and the types of books that build on those interests.

- Ask what they think you and they can do to help them become better readers.
- Stress that children who are not yet good readers are not "stupid." They just need to learn good reading strategies.
- Discuss the idea that using strategies can make reading easier and more fun.

## Teach and model good reading strategies.

Many children do not discover reading strategies on their own. Teacher's must teach strategies directly. Talk about what a strategy is and why it is important. Point out the following:

- Good readers set purposes for reading.
- Good readers look at titles, pictures, and graphics to help them figure out words.
- Good readers always try to make sense of what they read.

Stress that readers of all ability levels can learn and use these strategies. Explain and model **what** these strategies are, **how** they should be used, **why** they are important, and **when** they should be used.

Ask often: "What strategy should you use when you come to a word you do not know?" Encourage children to read an unfamiliar word as a blank, to finish the sentence, and then to come back to see what word would make sense. Also, connect these strategies to content-area reading in other parts of the curriculum.

## Explain the reading program and good reading strategies to family members.

- This can be done at a meeting or through a newsletter and will enable families to better help their children at home.
- Help parents and guardians understand that they play a crucial part in their children's learning and reading success.
- Stress the importance of encouraging children to read at home every day.

## Provide varied types of instruction.

- Whole-group instruction allows children to interact with other children and benefit from discussion.
- Small-group instruction enables the teacher to monitor reading progress and provide skills instruction in meaningful context.
- Individual instruction allows teachers to focus on individual needs and accomplishments.
- Listening centers are particularly helpful to auditory learners and to students acquiring English as a second language.
- Peer tutors enable students to learn from each other.

- Cooperative learning groups enable students to learn collaborative skills.

## Encourage prediction.

- Prediction sets purposes for reading.
- Encourage children to read to confirm their predictions, but stress that predictions cannot turn out "wrong." Children should feel free to change their predictions as they read.
- Prediction helps keep children on task. Children tend to stay focused when they are reading to find out what will happen next.

## Encourage risk-taking.

- Help children understand that making errors is a natural part of learning.
- Don't accept "I don't know" and "I can't." Respond with invitations such as "What do you think?" or "What's your best guess?"
- Give positive reinforcement whenever possible.
- Allow adequate "wait time" for children to answer questions. If they're stumped, rephrase your question.

## Engage in activities that produce confidence. Here are some examples:

- Read the text to children before expecting them to read it on their own.
- Use language experience stories based on children's interests.
- Use group activities such as shared reading, echo reading, choral reading, partner reading, and Readers Theatre. Repeated readings build confidence and help children focus on meaning. Use think-alouds during oral readings to model good reading strategies.
- Reread for expression and fluency.
- Reread children's favorite part of the story.

## Build on what is known.

- Encourage children to look at a familiar word to figure out an unfamiliar word. For example, if the unfamiliar word is small, write the word all, and say "You know this word." Have a child say the word. "Since this word is *all,* then this word must be _____."
- Connect learning to children's background experiences and interests.

## Teach vocabulary and skills in meaningful contexts.

- Teaching vocabulary and skills in meaningful context helps children make sense and purpose of the learning.
- Whenever possible, show an unfamiliar word in several different contexts.
- Teach skills such as sequence, main idea, and cause and effect as they relate to stories students have read *and* to "real-life" situations.

## Look for activities that older children can do with younger children.

- Children can share with younger children by reading to them, developing a puppet show about a story, writing stories together, and even modeling or teaching a lesson.

## Help children see evidence of their progress.

- Tape-record children as they read orally.
- Replay the tape in a month or so. Talk about the progress that has been made and what children notice about their reading. This is an excellent way for children, teachers, and children's families to monitor reading progress.
- Use the tape to determine the strategies the child is using and strategies that need to be further developed.

## Read aloud to children every day.

- Reading aloud models fluency.
- Reading aloud is an opportunity to model what good readers do.
- As children follow along in their copies of a story, words that they recognize orally become words they can recognize in print.
- You may wish to tape-record some of the stories you read. These tapes can be used by children in a listening center.

## Have students read silently every day.

- Often, reluctant readers are expected to read only orally. To become successful silent readers, these students must be given the opportunity to read silently.
  - In the beginning, ensure success by having students read a few pages at a time.
  - Ask meaningful questions to monitor comprehension.
  - Reading silently *before* reading aloud can help students focus on meaning rather than on performance.

# Gifted & Talented Students

**by Dr. W. Dorsey Hammond**

*Professor of Education, Oakland University, Rochester, Michigan*

Giftedness can take many forms. When we think of giftedness we often think of the intellectually gifted: those students scoring very high on an individually administered I.Q. test. Certainly, this is one type of giftedness. Within our classroom there may also be students gifted in the arts: the visual arts, drama, music, or dance for example. We often see students who are gifted writers or students who have the potential to become excellent writers. Other students are mathematically gifted or have a particular talent for science. Often we see students who are especially creative but do not score exceedingly high on achievement or intelligence tests. Other students are athletically gifted or talented. In today's schools, we often see students who are gifted with computers and technology. Thus, gifted and talented students may be very different from one another.

As teachers adjust their curriculum plans to meet the needs of gifted and talented students, they will do well to remember the following facts:

1. Students may be gifted in one area but not in another.
2. Gifted students are not always the highest achieving students.
3. Gifted students are not always the most socially mature.
4. Creative students may or may not be the most intellectually advanced.
5. Giftedness shows up at different levels of development; with some students, the gift is obvious; with other students, we see potential that needs nurturing and development.
6. Giftedness seldom develops to full potential without instruction, coaching and encouragement, mentoring, and modeling.

Because giftedness takes many forms, it is not possible to provide a prescription or a specific curriculum. However, here are some suggestions for realistic activities to engage gifted and talented students in the primary and intermediate grades.

# In the Primary Classroom

## For the child gifted with an extraordinary memory . . .

Provide comfortable, inviting settings for children to share what they have learned about a topic that interests them. Encourage them to use graphic organizers such as K-W-L charts and prediction charts as part of their presentation to a group. Since these children's interests may be quite sophisticated, you may need to coach them to keep their audience in mind as they plan what they will say and show, how they will explain it, and how they will keep their listeners interested.

## For the child gifted with a highly developed imagination . . .

All children eventually become bored with routine tasks, but gifted and talented children may reach a level of competency much sooner than their peers. When they're ready for something else to do, put them to work helping you! Some children might enjoy transforming a set of learning tasks into a game format; for example, making games for specific phonics skills. Encourage children to work with a partner to create game boards, game pieces, and rules for a game that will appeal to their classmates. Other children might prefer to research a topic in depth and plan a presentation—diorama, play, book— that makes good use of their talents.

## For the child gifted with unusual musical, artistic, or athletic ability . . .

Ask these children to help you plan and carry out a special literacy event based on their area of expertise. For example, a Literary Field Day might feature activity stations set up outdoors or in a gym. Each activity station represents one book the children know well. Small groups of children travel from station to station, completing a literature-based activity and receiving a badge for their efforts. By the end of the field day, everyone's a winner!

## For the child gifted with unusual writing or dramatic ability . . .

These children can help you establish and maintain two of your most important learning centers: the writing/publishing center and the dramatic play center. Ask children to work collaboratively on furnishing the centers with different props, depending on the stories the class is reading. These children can write and direct original plays, compile big books and poetry collections, present puppet shows, and write and illustrate books for younger children. These children can also be encouraged to help other children make comparisons and connections among books, themes, authors, illustrators, and so on.

## For the child gifted with unusual mathematical ability . . .

Don't forget the computer! Of course, children with all kinds of special talents can benefit from time on the computer, providing the software meets their needs and ability levels. But certain programs are particularly well suited to children whose ways of thinking about math concepts, patterns, and relationships are especially unique.

Every child presents us with new challenges and opportunities. Gifted and talented children enrich our entire classroom and make learning more exciting for everyone. Look for giftedness in every child; then do what you can to nurture and promote it!

# In the Intermediate Classrooms

### Long-Term Investigations

Encourage students to investigate an area of interest in depth, over a period of several weeks. The area of interest might be a topic such as space exploration, transportation, advertisement, technology, or government, or a political issue or historical event. Students may choose to study a prominent individual or do an author study. Such long-term activities promote sustained investigative skills: raising questions, researching answers, and organizing information.

### Original Stories

Writing is an excellent medium for promoting some types of giftedness. In addition to writing and revising stories, students can be encouraged to write an original play or to identify a favorite short story and rewrite it as a play or a television script. Encourage the study and writing of poetry and even songs. Suggest that students write and illustrate books for younger children. Writers, illustrators, and editors can collaborate and work together.

### Thought-Provoking Questions

When reading and discussing literature, ask questions that promote thoughtful responses. For example, "What is this story really about?" is a provocative question about themes. Encourage students to explore hypothetical story paths with questions such as "What might have happened if . . ." In addition, encourage students to make connections between books and authors. For example, "Of the two books by this author, which was a better book for you and why?" Encourage dialogue. Ask students to respond to the author's writing style as distinguished from the plot of the story. Encourage reflections on characters and how characters change. In summary, promote critical and thoughtful responses to allow students to demonstrate their giftedness and creativity.

### Diverse Reading

Encourage gifted students to read diversely and to read original sources. For example, when studying history, encourage students to read the writings and speeches of major historical figures such as Lincoln, King, and Jefferson as well as the writings of ordinary people in extraordinary circumstances.

### Problem-Solving

Pose problems in science and social studies. For example, "If you were heading out West in 1840 with a family of four and one wagon, what would you take with you, and why? What would you leave behind?" In science, involve students in hypothesizing and predicting and then testing their hypotheses. Raise questions with students. Raise issues. Students enjoy dealing with problem-solving situations.

### Collaboration

Encourage collaboration when appropriate. Students need to recognize not only their own gifts but also the giftedness of others. The abilities to work together, to assume leadership, and to take directions are forms of giftedness.

*The above suggestions are merely a few examples. Different students provide us with different challenges and opportunities. Gifted and talented students enrich our entire classroom and make learning more exciting for all students. Most likely, every student is gifted in some manner. The key for the teacher is to find the giftedness, to nurture it and promote it.*

# TEACHING SPEAKERS OF NONSTANDARD ENGLISH

## BY DR. ELEANOR W. THONIS • RETIRED DISTRICT PSYCHOLOGIST
### WHEATLAND SCHOOL DISTRICT IN CALIFORNIA; FORMER CHAIRPERSON OF IRA'S MULTILITERACY COMMITTEE

## Valuing Variant Forms of English

Students bring the language of their homes to the classroom; their social and cultural experiences are reflected in their speech. Teachers have a responsibility to accept both standard and nonstandard English in appropriate situations. Students who use nonstandard (sometimes called "variant") forms must receive encouragement for their home dialect and for the ideas carried by it. Variant speakers represent an expected range of differences that may be found among *all* students in *any* classroom. An instructional program that is planned to use the many strengths of variant forms—vivid expressions, creative descriptions, and unusual metaphors—will validate the language of the home and affirm the school's respect for the students as well as for their families.

To demonstrate that you value the language of the home and the community, try the following suggestions:

- Avoid efforts to eliminate nonstandard speech, since students may need to know and use both nonstandard and standard English as they live and grow in a multicultural world.
- Be sensitive to the context of language exchange between and among students.
- Encourage students to bring stories, proverbs, and verses from home to share with the class.
- Occasionally offer materials that contain conversations and descriptions in variant forms of English.
- In informal conversations, focus on the message in students' expressions, not on the words or accents themselves.
- Differentiate between the use of dialect and actual errors in speech.

# Promoting Excellence in Standard English

Although variant forms, or dialects, of English should certainly not be labeled "wrong," students as individuals can only be empowered by having both standard and nonstandard English at their command. In formal situations, especially in situations where students are being judged by strangers, standard English is an extremely useful tool. Knowing standard English will help students in future classrooms, on college applications, in job interviews, in business communications, in debates and speeches, and so on.

An introduction to the importance of standard English can begin with a discussion of formality. Different types of diction are appropriate in different situations. You might want to brainstorm lists like the following with students:

> **informal situations**
> baseball games
> phone conversations with friends
>
> **somewhat formal situations**
> classroom conversations
> holiday get-togethers
>
> **very formal situations**
> a speech to the school
> meeting the mayor
> a research report

Point out that just as students *behave* more formally in formal situations, they may want to speak more formally, too. The language students use around their closest friends is not necessarily the language they will want to use when they are speaking to a large group or to an adult they do not know well, or when they are writing research papers in school or letters and memos in their future careers.

Here are some activities you may want to try to promote excellence in standard English:

- Model standard English when speaking to students in response, without specifically pointing out the difference between standard and variant forms.
- Read aloud to students often, and discuss whether a piece sounds formal or informal in tone.
- Teach contractions in English *after* students have learned the complete forms. Help students see both shortened and complete forms together so that they may recognize their connectedness.
- Use choral reading and shared reading for oral practice and for pleasure.
- Arrange pairs or small groups of students to work together—including both standard and nonstandard speakers of English.
- Role-play formal and informal situations, and encourage students to use language appropriate to each situation.
- Invite a community leader to visit to discuss the importance of standard English in appropriate situations.

# Second-Language Acquisition

BY DR. STEPHEN KRASHEN
**Professor of Curriculum and Teaching,
University of Southern California**

Roger Brown gave this advice to parents who were interested in accelerating first-language development in their own children:

*"Believe that your child can understand more than he or she can say, and seek, above all, to communicate. To understand and be understood. To keep your minds fixed on the same target. In doing that, you will, without thinking about it, make a hundred or maybe a thousand alterations in your speech and action. Do not try to practice them as such. There is no set of rules of how to talk to a child that can even approach what you unconsciously know. If you concentrate on communicating, everything else will follow."*
[Brown (1977)]

Just as we all have the same digestive and visual systems, we all acquire language the same way. The process is simple. We acquire language when we understand the language input we receive from other people or from reading.

There is a great deal of evidence for this "input hypothesis." It includes studies that show that methods using more "comprehensible input" (language that students readily understand) are more effective than methods using less, and that those exposed to more comprehensible input outside of school acquire more and, thus, they understand more linguistic knowledge. The input hypothesis also claims that we do not acquire language by direct study—by memorizing vocabulary lists, learning rules of grammar, or speaking or writing. Rather, a large vocabulary, grammatical accuracy, and spoken and written fluency are the results of language acquisition—a result of getting comprehensible input—not the causes of language acquisition.

An important corollary of the input hypothesis is the claim that if the child is given enough comprehensible input, all the grammar rules and vocabulary that the child is ready to acquire will be present in the input. In other words, we do not need to worry that certain structures and words are included. If we present language acquirers with enough interesting messages, the language they are ready to acquire will be there.

If the input hypothesis is correct, helping students acquire language must involve, centrally, helping them get comprehensible input. There are two ways of making input more comprehensible: (1) by altering the language we use or (2) by providing context, or background knowledge.

## Altering the Language We Use

There is no doubt that we often alter our speech to make it easier to understand. We don't talk the same way to a friend as we do to a small child. When we are speaking to children, our speech is grammatically simpler and sometimes slower, and it contains fewer difficult words. Does this mean we should make a conscious effort to change our speech when talking to second-language acquirers? While it is a good idea to talk a bit slower and to use simpler speech, there are no exact procedures teachers should follow in trying to make their speech more comprehensible. We don't have to worry about using fewer relative clauses or making less use of complex tenses. What is crucial is to make sure that what you say is understood. There are many ways to do this, ranging from simply asking "Did you understand?" (the least precise way) to noting physical reactions (did the child's behavior indicate comprehension?).

If we monitor comprehension, the input hypothesis tells us, the appropriate structures and vocabulary will automatically be provided.

As with spoken input, reading materials need only be comprehensible and interesting to support language acquisition. They need not be "authentic" (written by native speakers for native speakers), and there is nothing inherently wrong with using texts written for second-language acquirers, as long as they are interesting and comprehensible.

## Supplying Context

Something we can do to make our input more comprehensible is to supply context. Numerous studies have shown that providing context has a dramatic effect on comprehensibility, and common sense confirms this. It is, for example, much easier to understand input in a second language when you have some idea of the subject matter. It is very hard to "eavesdrop" in a second language.

Even when little primary-language help is available, it can be very valuable. Consider the case of a class with three Korean-speaking students who know little English. They are progressing fairly well in mathematics because of good math instruction in their first language, and because math does not require a high level of language ability in early grades. Assume that we have a helper who speaks Korean but who is available only one morning per week for one hour. My suggestion is that we inform the helper what is to be studied the following week in social studies, for example. If it is the Civil War, the helper may use the one hour on Monday to provide the students with background information, in Korean, about the Civil War—who the combatants were, what the issues were, etc. This will make the following week's history lessons much more comprehensible.

### Pictures

When beginning language teachers use pictures with language, they are supplying context. Stories are made more comprehensible when teachers show students the pictures in the book.

### Physical Movement

That it provides context is the reason "total physical response" works so well (Asher, 1988). In this language-teaching method, teachers give students commands requiring a physical movement ("Stand up!"). In the early stages, the teacher models the actions, which makes the commands more comprehensible.

### Language Itself

As students become more proficient, the information provided by language itself can be used as context; unknown individual words and grammatical rules are acquired more readily if they occur in a message that is comprehensible, even in the absence of context provided by the real world.

### The First Language

A very powerful means of supplying context is to use the child's first language. Clear support for this idea comes from successful bilingual programs. A good education in their primary language and knowledge of subject matter help students become more successful in acquiring English, because these things make the input they get in English more comprehensible. Similarly, when we read newspapers in other languages, the input is more comprehensible because of the knowledge of the news we obtained through our first language.

### Self-Selected Reading

We combine the two ways of making input more comprehensible (supplying simpler input and context) when we encourage students to do self-selected free reading. When students read what they want to read, they select reading material that they find interesting and comprehensible. Better readers have a tendency to read "series" books, books by the same author and/or books on a single topic. Good readers may get hooked on the Sweet Valley or Power Ranger series, for example, or the works of Judy Blume or R. L. Stine. One interpretation of this phenomenon is that such "narrow reading" helps students become good readers. Reading about the same characters or themes provides context and helps make the input more comprehensible, and this increases language and literacy development.

We know that when students are allowed to read what they want to read, they don't simply select easy books. They choose books based on their interests. There is, in addition, evidence that children's choices change and develop as they continue to do self-selected reading, which broadens their knowledge of both languages and the world.

## What to Do: A Summary

1. Provide students with comprehensible input in the classroom. For beginners, use TPR (total physical response), pictures, and other types of context.

2. Don't be overly concerned with making your speech "simple." While it is a good idea to think about "toning down" your speech when speaking to limited-English-proficient students, if you keep your focus on communication, you will automatically change your speech to make it easier to understand.

3. Take advantage of the child's first language to make input more comprehensible. This can be done even if you do not speak that language. The best way is to provide a full bilingual education program. A helper (paraprofessional, older student) may also provide some background knowledge.

4. Encourage free voluntary reading, and allow students to read "narrowly."

It must be more than coincidence that the best way to help students acquire another language is also the easiest and most pleasant way for both teachers and students. Providing comprehensible input via interesting classroom activities and self-selected reading is a more pleasant—and a much more effective—support for language acquisition than grammar drills, error correction, and vocabulary lists. 🍎

## What Not to Do

1. Don't correct errors. The research literature clearly shows that correction of children's language is practically useless. Even for older students who understand grammar and who are highly literate, correction results in either no improvement or in very modest improvement that shows up primarily on tests in which students can be focused on form. Accuracy improves when children get more comprehensible input, especially through reading, not when their output is correct.

2. Don't teach grammar. The research literature on grammar teaching is consistent. Grammar teaching has little or no effect on acquisition. Even with older students who understand grammar and who expect and want it, the results are small gains on tests in which students can focus on grammatical correctness, and these gains are typically short-lived. We all want children to speak and write with maximum grammatical accuracy. The way to develop accuracy is not through grammar exercises, however, but through comprehensible input, especially through reading.

3. Don't teach vocabulary. According to research done at the University of Illinois, picking up vocabulary by reading is ten times as efficient, in terms of words learned per minute, as learning through direct vocabulary instruction. Time is therefore better spent in reading. Pre-teaching vocabulary is also not very efficient. According to research, pre-teaching concepts provides context and is a big help in making input more comprehensible, but preteaching individual words is much less helpful. Besides, if a text or activity requires a great deal of preteaching, it is probably inappropriate.

# Support
## for Teachers of
## Students Acquiring
# ENGLISH

### by Eleanor W. Thonis

Everyone appears to agree that some modification must be made to accommodate second-language learners. The resource of the school, however, vary greatly from region to region and are not always available to support teachers or children in these efforts. To the extent that the means permit, teachers may benefit from opportunities to attend conferences, workshops, and other professional growth activities.

In the classroom, certain adaptations can make the learning more accessible and relieve the anxieties of children whose home language is different from the language of the school. This article provides practical suggestions for helping second-language children in the classroom. The suggestions fall into one or more of these categories: appreciating the home culture and language, classroom management techniques, and literacy activities.

## Appreciating the Home Culture and Language

- Ask children to teach to classmates words of greeting and common phrases from their home language.

- Identify aspects of the children's cultural experiences to use when they write—celebrating national events, welcoming the new year, preparing for birthdays, and so on.

- Invite family members to share their stories, music, art, legends, and folklore. You might also ask them to share their talents in the classroom, demonstrating needlework, origami, and so on.

- Provide literacy activities in the home language with the help of a teacher, parent, or other volunteer who knows both English and the home language.

## Classroom Management Techniques

- Provide frequent opportunities for children to communicate in simple English.

- Invite children to work in cooperative groups or in pairs to increase their comfort level and comprehension.

- Be certain that each small group has at least one child who can serve as a mentor or an interpreter.

- Set aside a small part of the classroom where children may go to find material on various reading levels, including some books in the home language.

## Literacy Activities

- Use objects, pictures, and posters to encourage small-group or whole-class discussion.

- Arrange centers that are specially equipped for listening, speaking, writing, and reading in the home language and in English.

- Take children on a short walking trip to a store, bank, or post office. Have children help you plan how to get there and what to do; then discuss the trip after returning to class.

- Continue to use predictable books for newcomers to English print.

- Do choral reading, and encourage children to retell parts of the story.

- Use a song that children know, and write some part of it on the board for the children to sing along.

- Suggest that children write stories using whatever language they wish. Encourage them to illustrate the stories.

- Bring in recipes in English for favorite dishes from children's home culture, and prepare simple dishes as a class.

- Collect examples of humor in cartoons or pictures that may be enjoyed in the home language.

- Ask children to suggest a word that is interesting or difficult to say; then have them explore the word's meaning in a variety of contexts. 🍎

# Fostering
# HOME LANGUAGE MAINTENANCE

## by Dr. Alma Flor Ada
**Professor and Director of the Center for Multicultural Literature for Children and Young Adults University of San Francisco**

Maintaining the ability to speak the language of their families will provide students with academic and professional assets in the future. Fostering a successful interaction with members of their culture strengthens students' sense of identity and gives them a firm platform from which to grow.

Unfortunately, most children who grow up in the United States speaking home languages other than English lose the ability to speak their mother tongues to a greater or lesser degree. They very seldom develop full literacy in their home languages.

This process not only leads to the loss of valuable abilities; it also causes children's sense of identity and self-esteem to suffer, and their relationships with their parents as well.

Education can determine the degree to which students maintain or lose their home languages. Maintaining the home language does not require the teacher speaking that language. Of course, a good bilingual program is the ideal situation for a student's abilities in the home language to grow and develop. But even within a nonbilingual classroom, a teacher who does not speak the language of the child can facilitate its maintenance and growth.

Students will feel better about their language if they see it related to prestigious activities; thus it is important to have students use the home language by acting as interpreters, translators, researchers, and teachers. Here are some activities that can be carried out at any level.

## 1. Book Sharing
Encourage students to take home books in the home language and to read them with their families or to have a family member read the books to them. Students can discuss the books with their families and record comments to share with the next student who borrows that book.

## 2. Written Translations
If students are literate in their home language, encourage them to translate appropriate books from their home language into English. Parents or other family members may be asked to help with translating. Have students bind and illustrate their books, displaying their own names as translators on the covers.

### 3. Development of Interpreting Skills

Show appreciation for students' translating or interpreting skills. Ask students to serve as interpreters for visitors, community members, or elders. Invite bilingual children to interview or to translate interviews with monolingual children in the class.

### 4. Students as Researchers

Encourage students to discuss with their parents what they are learning in school, using their home languages. Ask students to share their parents' feedback with the class.

### 5. Students as Storytellers

Have students ask their families to write or share the family's history and illustrate it with photos and artifacts. Students can then share the history with the class.

### 6. Students as Teachers

Encourage children to teach everyone in the class a few phrases or sentences in their home language. Have everyone learn to say "hello," "good-bye," "thank you," and "please" in every language represented in the class. Incorporate these expressions into everyday classroom conversations, and add new ones as appropriate.

### 7. International Chorus

Have children learn a song or poem in their home language and teach it to the class.

### 8. Building Bridges

Provide editions in students' home languages of the literature books you are studying or reading with the whole class. Let students read, or at least find in the book, some words they recognize in their home language. (In some languages they may be able to find word cognates with similar spellings in two languages, e.g., *kilo*.) Have students take the books home and share them with their families. 🍎

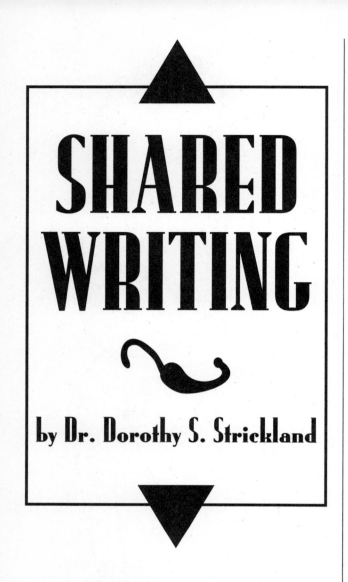

# SHARED WRITING

## by Dr. Dorothy S. Strickland

"If we want Ashley's mom to come and show us how to plant our garden, how can we let her know?" Janiece Turner looked out at her second graders as hands flew in the air to respond.

"Ask Ashley to tell her," replied Josh.

"Call her up," answered Angel.

"Is there anything else we might do?" asked Janiece.

"Well, I guess we could write her a letter," Tonya responded.

"We certainly could," said Janiece. "And we can do it together."

Janiece went to the easel, flipped to a clean sheet of chart paper, and began an interactive process in which she and the children went back and forth, making decisions about what to say, how it might be spelled, and where it should go.

"How do we start?"

Someone suggested *Dear Mrs. Benton*.

"Does anyone besides Ashley know how *Benton* begins?"

"Yes, with a *B*," someone offered.

"Good, James. Will you spell the rest of your name for us, Ashley? Notice that I'm putting a comma after *Benton*. Now, it would be very nice to include the date on our letter. Does anyone have any idea where we should put it? Who can help us spell *March?*"

The process continues until a draft of the letter is completed. The children review what they have said. Janiece asks for comments about changes. Later, she will enter the letter in the computer and have one or two children decorate the stationery before it goes home with Ashley. Janiece will hang the draft in the library corner for the children to read at their leisure.

> "Shared writing provides a risk-free opportunity for children to engage in the writing process."

## What is shared writing?

Shared writing is an interactive group writing process in which teachers and children work together to compose or record meaningful messages and stories. The teacher often acts as a scribe as he or she thinks through with children what they want to say and the best way to say it. Individual children may also act as scribes as they fill in letters and words that they know. Everyone works together to draft, revise, and edit as appropriate. Shared writing provides a risk-free opportunity for children to engage in the writing process.

Any kind of writing may be the focus of shared writing: response to reading, group stories, big books, poems, informational notes and books, class charts, and written retellings are just a few.

# Why is shared writing important?

- Writing is shown to be a functional, meaningful way to communicate.
- Teachers model reading and writing during the creation of the text.
- The entire writing process, from brainstorming during prewriting to proofreading and editing, may be modeled to the extent that it is appropriate.
- A variety of writing strategies are developed as children get firsthand demonstrations and rehearsal from participating with others.
- Specific skills may be explained in context as children help to produce a finished piece.

# What happens during shared writing?

## Prewriting

**Stimulus**   Shared writing is generally stimulated by a common experience of some kind, such as a class trip, a school assembly, or a book that the teacher has read aloud to the whole group.

**Discussion**   Actual writing is usually preceded by a brief discussion: Who is our audience? What form of writing should we use? What should we say?

## Drafting

**Writing**   The teacher guides children as they "think through" the process together. The teacher acts as a scribe, demonstrates the conventions of writing, and uses prompts to help children explore possible ideas for their text.

## Revision/Proofreading

**Refining**   Throughout the writing, the teacher constantly solicits help by asking questions and thinking aloud about needed wording, punctuation, spelling, and so on. Upon completion of the piece, the teacher and children review it together for final polishing.

## OPPORTUNITIES FOR SHARED WRITING

- Group retellings
    Story read aloud
    Facts remembered from a nonfiction text
- Group compositions
    Original stories
    Big books
    Alternative texts based on stories read aloud
    Poetry
- Class charts
    Class jobs
    Class rules
    Directions
- Captions for displays
    Books by Cynthia Rylant
    Shells found on the beach
    Our baby pictures

Dear Mrs. Benton,

# Writing in the Classroom

**by Evelyn Cudd** *Teacher, Rock Prairie School, College Station, Texas*

These are some questions that teachers often ask about writing, along with answers I have gleaned from the research and my own experience.

**Q** **I have read so much about teaching writing in the last five years that I find myself going in a hundred different directions with my lessons. I'm confusing myself and my students. What is important to teach in writing?**

**A** First of all, it may be helpful to keep in mind the four elements of effective writing:

1. **Focus:** the clarity with which the piece presents a main idea, point of view, theme, or important event; and the exclusion of irrelevant information

2. **Organization:** the overall plan of development (beginning, middle, ending); the logical relationship of ideas; and the use of transitional devices

3. **Elaboration:** the quality of detail or support; the use of examples or reasons clearly related to the topic; word choice, specificity, depth, accuracy, credibility, and completeness

4. **Conventions:** punctuation, capitalization, spelling, usage, and grammar

These four elements are frequently used as criteria for evaluation of effective writing and can be easily remembered and understood by students. The elements provide a general structure from which to select topics for minilessons or for longer instructional periods. For example, students frequently omit transitional devices between events in a narrative. (Johnny is driving down the road with his family and in the next sentence he is swimming in the ocean.) When you work with students on this problem, refer to the four elements and discuss the problem as an organizational lapse. In this way, students begin to understand more fully that organization entails more than a beginning, a middle, and an ending.

**Q** **I am confused about self-selected topics for writing. Is there ever a time when it's legitimate to assign a topic?**

**A** There is nothing pedagogically unsound about assigning a topic. In fact, research indicates that the most effective writing program is one that contains a mix of self-selected and assigned topics. What is unsound is assigning a topic or handing children a story starter without providing for discussion and planning. Remember also that an assigned topic usually has an element of choice. If you ask students to write about a memorable moment in their lives, they choose the moment.

**Q** I've been hearing and reading a lot about product versus process. If I don't emphasize product, many of my students won't ever complete a piece. What's a proper balance?

**A** When students understand the process that writers go through to bring a piece of writing to completion, they can improve the quality of their writing. Knowledge of this process alone, however, is not sufficient. Students must be expected to demonstrate a working knowledge of the process that culminates in published pieces. It is difficult to give an exact number, but I generally expect my students to publish one major piece about every six weeks.

The product issue has another aspect. Process writing is only one part of an effective writing program. Students should be writing for a variety of purposes every day, for example, note-taking and writing in response journals and learning logs. The writing done for these purposes is a product.

Students should also receive direct instruction in writing each day. These lessons can be minilessons or expanded lessons, and some type of product or evidence of transfer should usually be expected from students after the lesson. For instance, if you give a minilesson on sentence combining, a reasonable expectation would be for the students to choose two or three sentences from their work and combine them. This is a product. Most products are not fully process pieces.

**Q** I have students who refuse to write. What can I do to get them to pick up their pencils and try?

**A** One of the most effective ways to get children to write is through having them do written retellings of short, familiar folktales, fables, or simple books like Esphyr Slobodkina's *Caps for Sale*. Retellings simply remove the risk of failure by allowing children to use good writing as a model. When they retell a story, they practice using the vocabulary, organization, and style of the model. Once children are writing, their confidence and fluency begin to increase. The basic steps for retelling follow:

1. Read and discuss the selection.
2. Draw attention to the organization of the selection, to effective word choice, and to special techniques, such as repetition.
3. Model a written retelling on the board or on an overhead.
4. Have students write their own retelling. This can be done collaboratively or individually.

**Q** I hear the term *writer's workshop* a lot. How do I start a writer's workshop with my students?

**A** There are many different kinds of writer's workshops, but they all involve setting aside periods of time for writing, preferably every day. During the workshop, students use the writing process (prewriting, drafting, responding and revising, editing and proofreading, and publishing), although it is important for them to understand that they can move back and forth, at their own pace, among the components of the process.

Students might find their topics through reading and discussing literature, through group and individual brainstorming, or through looking back at their own journals for ideas. They should get feedback from each other and from the teacher through conferences. At "teachable moments" during the editing and proofreading stages, the teacher may present a minilesson in grammar, mechanics, spelling, or a related area. One important feature of the writer's workshop is the opportunity for students to publish their work and thereby receive recognition for their efforts.

**Q** I know that process writing is important, but I don't want my children to have to take every piece of writing through all the stages. Is there one stage that shouldn't be skipped?

**A** Prewriting is considered by many experts to be the most important stage of the writing process and the stage on which more of the writing time should be spent. The quality of children's writing that ensues is directly related to what goes on during this time. During this stage, children decide on purpose, form, and audience. They generate ideas about a topic and ways to organize those ideas. It is also a time for teacher modeling or collaborative compositions. Even if the writing goes no further, a great deal is learned about writing during this stage.

**Q** What do I do with "hopeless" pieces that are only a few lines long and contain so many errors in syntax and mechanics that they are difficult to read and impossible to respond to in a positive way?

**A** Research indicates that most responses to lower-level pieces are in the form of suggestions concerning spelling and mechanics. This should be avoided completely. It only discourages and further stifles any possibility for improvement in writing. Instead, focus on content. Ask questions about the piece that show an interest in the writer's thoughts. The power of personal interest and sincere questions should never be underestimated.

**Q** Some authorities have recommended that handwriting no longer be taught. I feel that handwriting is important. What is your opinion?

**A** The problem with formal instruction in handwriting is not the instruction itself, but the endless copying of specific writing exercises from the board or from dittos. This kind of practice inevitably leads to less time for meaningful writing, and its effect on letter formation and legibility is dubious.

It is important to demonstrate the correct formation of letters in manuscript and of cursive and letter connections if you are working with cursive. This can be accomplished in minilessons followed by short, guided practices. Once the letter formation has been learned, there is no justification for any handwriting practice as an end in itself.

Children should be taught that legibility is part of written communication. Opportunities for practicing handwriting should be accomplished through purposeful writing, not meaningless exercises.

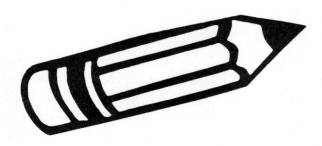

# Stages in Emergent Writing

## by Patricia Smith

**Not long ago, many educators believed children had to be well versed in reading and "readiness" skills before they could write. We now know these facts:**

- Children know much more about print at an earlier age than we gave them credit for in the past.

- Children discover that writing is oral language in written form. What can be said can also be written.

- Emergent writers experiment with writing long before they're independent readers, and what they learn about print from shared reading is reflected in what and how they write. Reading and writing develop together.

- Young children who see writing modeled at home and at school are eager to try it on their own and quickly come to view themselves as writers with something important to say.

Beginning writers progress through predictable, recognizable stages that will vary in duration for individual children. Since these stages are not rigid, examples from more than one of the following stages will often appear in the same piece of writing:

1. **Pre-alphabetic** scribbling, or pretend writing, is not necessarily random marks on the page (Figure 1). It may be a child's first attempt to approximate the print he or she encounters naturally all day long. Listen for the running monologue that may accompany a child's scribbling; this child is well aware that written symbols contain meaning!

2. **Alphabetic** letter strings, or random letters, are a child's attempts to mimic the forms of our alphabet (Figure 2). At this pre-phonemic stage, letters do not yet represent sounds. More often than not, the child uses capital letters. You may notice that a child at this stage is already practicing left-to-right and top-to-bottom progression on the page.

3. **Early Phonetic** one-letter spelling is a common occurrence in the early phonemic stage (Figure 3). Here a child uses the initial consonant, and perhaps another distinctive consonant, to represent an entire word, such as *b* for *baby* or *bl* for *believe*.

4. **Phonetic** invented spelling is a window on a child's understanding of sound-symbol correspondences (Figure 4). Children who are encouraged to "spell a word the best they can" experiment with beginning and ending consonants and often with medial sounds as well. Usually, vowels come much later although all-important words like *I* and *a* appear early in a child's writing vocabulary.

5. **Transitional** spelling is the stage in which children adjust their own simple spelling rules (*shz* for *shoes, wans* for *once*) to accommodate what they're learning from their reading (Figure 5). Features such as double consonants and silent letters also begin to appear.

6. **Conventional** spelling begins to appear in a few high-frequency words written by young primary children. As these children continue through the primary grades, more words are written with conventional spelling.

Figure 1

Figure 2

Figure 3

Figure 4

Figure 5

## Promoting Conventional Spelling

Consider developing a poster with the following information to support conventional spelling.

### SPELLING STEPS

1. Say the word softly.
2. Think of the sounds you hear.
3. Write the word.
4. Look at your word.
5. Make changes if it does not look right.
6. Look at it again. If it appears right, go on. If not . . .
7. Use help from
   - a place where the word is already printed.
   - a person who can help you spell the word.
8. Write the word correctly on your paper and in your spelling journal.

### Keep in Mind . . .

Remember that we want our children to use the best words they can think of, even if they are unable to spell the words correctly. Reassure chidden that you will be able to read or hear them read what they have written. Tell children that having their thoughts in written form is what you want *most of all.*

When it appears that children are moving into transitional and conventional spelling, you can support their spelling efforts by

- allowing children to help one another achieve more conventional spelling.
- teaching the correct spelling of high-frequency words.
- creating a print-rich environment that includes banks of words that might be used in writing.

- supplying children with personal spelling journals in which they can write new words on alphabetized pages.
- showing children how to circle in early drafts the words with which they want spelling assistance.
- reassuring children that while you are proud of their growing spelling abilities, you understand that they may not be able to spell the words used by older writers.

---

### Management Tip

Trim chart paper with width of a coat hanger. Let children attach their own word banks to hangers. Hang the word banks in the coat closet for easy storage and retrieval when needed. The charts can be hung near children who need the spelling help.

Some children have extensive experience with writing before they enter school; others may be experimenting with crayons and pencils for the first time. You can promote children's emergent writing by

- modeling writing behaviors every day.
- providing writing supplies in learning centers.
- encouraging children to make their own signs, lists, recording sheets, captions, and so on when they need them.
- setting aside time for children to keep personal journals, to write individual and group stories, and to respond to literature in writing.
- celebrating the efforts of emergent writers.

# STRATEGIES

## PREWRITING

**by Evelyn Cudd — Teacher, Rock Prairie School, College Station, Texas**

*Examples of questions teachers ask about the use of prewriting.*

**Q** I know that process writing is important, but I don't want my students to have to take every piece of writing through all the stages. They will just get burned out and so will I. Is there one stage of the writing process that is more important than the others and shouldn't be skipped?

**A** Prewriting is considered by many experts to be the most important stage of the writing process. The quality of student writing that ensues is directly related to what goes on during this time. During the prewriting stage, students decide on purpose, form, and audience. They generate ideas about a topic and ways to organize those ideas. It is also a time for teacher modeling and collaborative composition. Even if the writing goes no further, a great deal is learned about writing during this stage.

**Q** I always spend time generating ideas with my students before they begin writing, but their good ideas are often disorganized or rambling when they write. What can I do to help?

**A** Prewriting is not only a time for generating ideas but also a time when organization should be considered. Depending on the purpose of the writing, different organizational patterns can be considered. Clustering supporting ideas around main points is one way to graphically organize information. A chain-of-events organizer is helpful for stories.

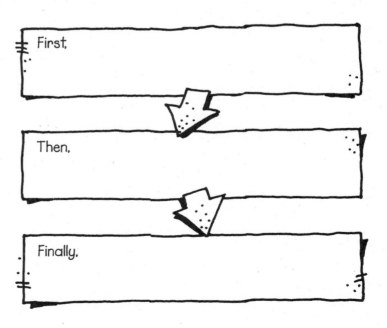

First,

Then,

Finally,

**Q** I know that note-taking is one prewriting activity, but I have a hard time getting my students to take notes and use them in their writing. How can I get my students started on note-taking?

**A** As students read or listen to informational selections, listen to guest speakers, or watch filmstrips or videotapes, have them jot down the new things they are learning. Model this procedure yourself, pointing out that you are writing down key words or phrases, not complete sentences. Students can then use what they have jotted down to write a paragraph about the new information. It is easiest to begin note-taking with content-area reading selections. After discussing with students what they already know about a topic, have them begin reading and taking notes on new learning. This can include jotting down page and paragraph numbers, especially for students with motor problems. Discussion and follow-up writing is then guided by the notes.

**Q** How can I get my students to take real notes rather than copy information verbatim from resource books?

**A** Try using a **QUAD**, an acronym for **qu**estions, **a**nswers, **d**etails. Students select a topic and create a grid. Next, they write at least four to five questions about the topic. It is important that they write the questions before they use resource books. Finally, they go to the Media Center with their grids and research the answers. A K-W-L chart works in much the same way; students write what they *know*, what they *want* to know, and, after reading, what they *learned*. Since students are answering specific questions, the reading and the writing are purposeful.

**Q** One suggestion I frequently hear for prewriting is teacher modeling. This takes so much time. How important is it?

**A** It is not necessary for a teacher to model every writing assignment, but teacher modeling should be a regular part of your writing instruction. Students frequently do not understand verbal descriptions, even when accompanied with clusters, frames, or other visuals. They need more specific examples or models of how to put their ideas on paper.

For example, if you are asking students to write a personal narrative about an exciting moment in their lives, you might model a lead, including the setting of the incident or events leading up to it, followed by an account of what happened and the reactions of those around you, and ending with reflections on why you were excited. This modeling can be coupled with a "write aloud," in which the teacher writes while talking about his or her writing, including thoughts on organization and possible spots where examples or anecdotes might be appropriate to clarify or illustrate points.

# ACTIVITIES

## PREWRITING

*Prewriting is the most important step in the writing process. Here are some prewriting activities to add to your collection of tried-and-true favorites:*

### For Narrative and Creative Writing

- Draw.
- Brainstorm.
- Look through your journals.
- Visualize a scene.
- Go to the classroom Idea File.
- Fill in this diagram:

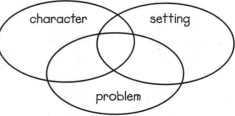

character   setting

problem

### For Expository Writing

- Make a time line.
- Make a chart to record your data.
- Have a conference to narrow your topic.
- Fill in a planning chart:

| What I Know | What I Want to Find Out |
|---|---|
|  |  |

- Fill in a chart that compares:

| ME | A BIRD |
|---|---|
| can run | can run |
| can sing | can sing |
| can't fly | can fly |

## For Descriptive Writing

- Draw it.
- Talk about it.
- Move like the person, animal, or object.
- Make a chart that tells about it:

  | what I saw |
  |---|
  | what I heard |
  | what I felt |

- Make a word web:

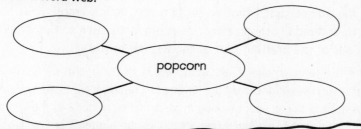

## What the teacher can provide

- daily scheduled time(s) for writing
- an "inspiration corner"
- a file box or bulletin board where everyone contributes ideas
- occasional guided imagery experiences for the whole group
- minilessons during small-group or individual conferences
- a role model of someone who writes to learn, writes for pleasure, writes to get things done

# DRAFTING STRATEGIES

by Dr. Timothy Shanahan, Professor of Urban Education,
University of Illinois, Chicago

*Some questions often-heard regarding the drafting stage of the writing process.*

**Q** Most of the advice that I find on writing instruction emphasizes prewriting or revision. How should I organize my classroom instruction so that students will get the most out of the drafting part of the writing process?

**A** Although it is often easier to think about how to help students before or after writing, teachers can successfully facilitate the writing or drafting itself in many ways. One of the first things to do is to talk about writing in ways that offer students the appropriate mindset. For instance, poet Alan Ziegler doesn't talk about "writing" or "composing" with his students. He talks about "exploratory writing." In exploratory writing, students are just finding out what they know by writing down their ideas. This notion of exploring ideas is less formidable for most students, and it more accurately describes the process. Referring to student compositions as "drafts" rather than as stories or reports at this stage can help reduce the pressure to produce polished prose the first time.

It is also helpful if drafting can be a regularly scheduled classroom activity. Not only do students improve with practice, but they have a chance to be mentally prepared if they know ahead of time that they will be writing. It is also a good idea to try to make this writing time relatively quiet and uninterrupted. Writing is hard enough without unnecessary distractions. Finally, encourage students to ignore their errors at this point. If they are uncomfortable with this, especially at first, ask them to underline or circle the errors and just keep writing.

**Q** We often use brainstorming as a prewriting technique in my fifth-grade classroom. How should students use their brainstormed lists and charts during drafting?

**A** It's often best just to set those aside and write. Sometimes writers get so tied up in their lists that they have trouble going beyond them. Prewriting activities should help students think and make them aware of what they want to say. The lists themselves often don't have any value. It might be a good idea to have your students put that material away and refer to it only as needed or use it to check against their drafts when they are done. (This approach can also be helpful with other types of prewriting activities, such as research for an article or report. Having the research material at hand often encourages students to read rather than write, or to copy rather than draft. If it is out of sight, the writing—and the learning—improves.)

**Q** Some of my third graders will write a little bit and spend a lot of time trying to change what they have written. They never seem to get anything drafted. What can I do?

**A** Nancie Atwell, author of *In the Middle,* has a rule in her classroom: No erasing. If her students want to change something, they can cross it out quickly and keep going. She does that so she has a complete record of the students' ideas. However, this rule can reduce a lot of unnecessary off-task time as well, and it keeps students drafting rather than revising. The "no erasing" rule might be a good one for your classroom.

**Q** What should I do if one of my fourth-grade students has writer's block and just can't seem to get anything drafted?

**A** Songwriter Randy Newman once announced at a concert: "What am I doing here? I'm a writer. I should be home worrying about not writing." Most writers get blocked from time to time, a very frustrating situation for both student and teacher. Writers try all kinds of strategies to get themselves drafting. These strategies all work—some of the time. You might consider encouraging students to write nonstop for a fixed amount of time while a preset timer runs. It can be easier to keep writing for 12 minutes or 18 minutes than to write something in particular. If students get stuck for

an idea, they should rewrite their last sentence over and over until they get another idea. That keeps them writing and encourages them to think while they write. Rarely do students need to rewrite more than a sentence or two.

Sometimes students get blocked by the loneliness of the writing situation. It often helps to have them try to write their story or article in the form of a letter to themselves or to a friend. That can be a less lonely approach, and the student can revise the draft later. It also helps to switch writing tools or papers in some cases. Being able to choose from a variety of pens, pencils, markers, and papers can sometimes be enough motivation to get a writer back on track.

**Q** Any other ideas for helping my students to get better at drafting?

**A** It's a good idea to talk with students about their writing from time to time. Reflections on drafting—when the drafting is effective and going smoothly—can provide valuable insights. These insights will be useful when students confront a more challenging writing situation. Ask your students questions such as these: How did your drafting go today? Did your ideas come all at once during writing, or did they arise in some other way? Did anyone have trouble getting going? What did you do?

# STRATEGIES

## RESPONDING AND REVISING

### by Evelyn Cudd — Teacher, Rock Prairie School, College Station, Texas

*Some often-asked questions about getting students to respond to feedback and to revise their writing.*

**Q** **What is a quick way to respond to students' writing without resorting to lengthy written comments?**

**A** Keeping in mind that, to be effective, responses should be specific, I find that taking a highlighter and highlighting favorite parts or especially effective sections works very well. The teacher or the student's peers might highlight a well-chosen word or an effective simile, a strong lead, or an effective transition.

**Q** **What do I do with "hopeless" pieces that are only a few lines long and contain so many errors in syntax and mechanics that they are difficult to read and impossible to respond to in a positive way?**

**A** Research indicates that most responses to lower-level pieces are in the form of suggestions concerning spelling and mechanics. This should be avoided completely. It will only discourage and further stifle any possibility for improvement in writing. Instead, focus on content. Ask questions about the piece that show an interest in the author's thoughts, even if those thoughts have been expressed in sentence fragments with almost impossible spelling. The power of personal interest and sincere questions should never be underestimated. For instance, if Brendan has written *my dog he big we is friends,* his teacher might say, "When I read your story, I wondered about how you and your dog became friends. Was he a gift? What did you think the first time you saw him?" As Brendan begins to respond and talk about his story, he gains confidence in himself and begins to trust the teacher not to humiliate him.

**Q** When my students revise, the revisions don't seem to make any difference in the quality of the work. The paper is just cleaned up. How can I get my students to understand that revision means improving quality?

**A** Teach the difference between revision and editing. Demonstrate with class papers or with your own work. Discuss the kind of thinking that is involved in revision and the kind of thinking involved in editing. Show examples of papers that have been revised and discuss improvement in quality. Take one of the same papers and just edit it. Contrast the quality of the simply edited piece with the quality of the revised piece.

**Q** What does research say about computers and revision? How helpful are computers and word processing programs in assisting children to revise?

**A** Much more research in this area is needed, but at this point it appears that children who use word processors tend to edit, or correct errors in spelling, mechanics, and grammar, more than students who use pen and paper; however, the overall quality of the writing does not improve, because only editing has occurred, not revision. Expanded revision on more than the word or phrase level appears to occur more often when the student uses pen and paper than when word processors are used.

**Q** How do I teach my children to revise? They just can't seem to distance themselves from their work enough to make needed changes. Even sharing in writing groups hasn't really helped them to make substantive changes.

**A** One of the most effective techniques for teaching revision is through group revision lessons, as shown in the following steps:

**STEP 1** Choose a generic topic for writing; for example, a special friend or a trip. After prewriting and drafting, collect student papers.

**STEP 2** Choose one major problem on which to concentrate. Major areas include focus, organization, and elaboration.

**STEP 3** Choose papers from your class or other classes that exemplify the problem; for example, lack of elaboration. It's a good idea to begin a collection of papers that illustrate particular problems. Be careful not to choose papers that have other major flaws. If you are focusing on elaboration, choose papers that are organized and focus on the topic but that lack adequate examples or anecdotes to develop the topic properly. Praise the effective parts of the paper before pointing out needed improvements.

**STEP 4** Discuss each paper, beginning with the lowest-level paper. For example, if you are focusing on elaboration, you could begin with an organized list. Move to another paper with one or two details or examples, and so on, until you discuss a paper with a topic that is well-elaborated. (Four or five papers are sufficient.) Students should begin to identify the details that have been elaborated on and note where more elaboration is needed to develop a point or clarify an idea.

**STEP 5** Ask students to write again on the same topic, remembering what you have just discussed and shown examples of. Do not hand back their original papers.

**STEP 6** The next day, hand back the original paper with the revised paper. Ask students to compare the two papers.

This kind of lesson helps students begin to focus on more than superficial errors. They begin to identify and label major problems in writing, by recognizing them first in other students' work and then in their own work. By not handing back the original papers to the students, you have given them the distance needed for substantive change.

Working with group revision and focusing on major problem areas create a common body of knowledge and vocabulary that facilitates peer and teacher conferencing and leads to higher-level revision and improvement of quality.

# STRATEGIES
## PUBLISHING

**by Evelyn Cudd — Teacher, Rock Prairie School, College Station, Texas**

*Some questions about publishing students' work.*

**Q** What qualifies as a "published piece"? Do I have to word-process and bind my students' work for it to be published?

**A** Publishing student work can take many forms. This is a time when writing is shared publicly, orally or in a visual display. Publication can be as simple as writing a mathematical word problem composed by a student on the board with the byline "by Mashira," or as complex as entering a piece in an essay contest or binding the piece into a book for the classroom library. Publishing is synonymous with sharing and celebrating. It need not be elaborate to be effective.

**Q** Does all published work have to be error-free? If children do their own editing, they will not catch all the errors.

**A** The level of editing necessary depends upon the type of publication. If a child is submitting a piece of work for publication in a magazine, certainly editing assistance from the teacher is in order. Similarly, if your class is putting together a school newspaper, a chief editor is necessary. You can explain that book, magazine, and newspaper publishers all have editors who check for errors. When a child is sharing in an informal setting, absolute correctness is not required.

Here are a few publishing ideas:

**GROUP BOOK** Have several students bind their writing and art between paper or cardboard covers, or in a decorated loose-leaf notebook. Allow students to borrow the book overnight to share with their families.

**STUDENT OR TEACHER READ-ALOUD** The teacher, the author, or another student can read a piece aloud, with or without music, props, or a costume.

**STORY HOUR** Allow students to read their stories to groups of younger children.

**POETRY MURAL** If several students create poems or other short pieces on the same broad topic, have them make a mural on which to mount the pieces.

**READERS' THEATRE** Students' stories or plays can be read aloud as drama, with each character and the narrator played by a different student.

**TAPE RECORDINGS** Encourage students to tape-record their stories and listen to them later. You could even keep a small collection of students' tapes for class use.

**AUTHOR'S CHAIR** Designate one chair for the "author of the day" to sit in as he or she shares a piece of writing.

**FAMILY GIFTS** Students can make their writing into greeting cards, books, posters, and even bookmarks to give as special gifts to family members.

# FOR THE LOVE *of* READING

by **Dr. Bernice E. Cullinan**

*Professor of Early Childhood and Elementary
Education, New York University*

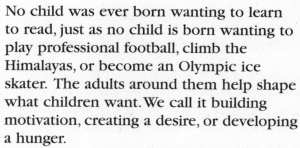

No child was ever born wanting to learn to read, just as no child is born wanting to play professional football, climb the Himalayas, or become an Olympic ice skater. The adults around them help shape what children want. We call it building motivation, creating a desire, or developing a hunger.

We entice children to learn to read by reading to them—engaging stories, compelling facts, and ridiculous rhymes. If parents have done their job well by reading to children during the preschool years, the children come to school yearning to read. These children understand that reading is worth the effort, that it proceeds from left to right across the page, and that some words begin with the same letter. They are off and running, eager to devour print and to try their hands at creating it.

If, however, children come to school without the basic background knowledge that wonderful things come from books, you need to start there—reading aloud, reading together, singing songs, and saying rhymes as a group. These endeavors not only help children learn how to read but also encourage them to want to read.

The materials you select can help ease children into the reading habit. For example, books with strong repetitive, rhythmic, and rhyming language will help children break the code easily. The words sound the way children think they should and match the sounds children expect to hear. Words that sound alike most often look alike, too; children recognize the similarity in spelling patterns quickly.

Rhyming words, patterned language, and rhythmic texts create what we call "predictable" texts because readers are able to predict what is coming next in the sentence. If you were to say

*"Pease porridge hot / Pease porridge cold
Pease porridge in the pot / Nine days ...,"*

Children would yell out "old!"

If you were to say

*"Humpty Dumpty sat on a wall.
Humpty Dumpty had a great ..."*

Children would say "fall."

If you were to read *Henny Penny,* children would soon join in to say with you,

*"Oh, Ducky Lucky! The sky is falling.
And we are going to tell the king."*

If you were to read "Five Little Ducks," children would sing and say the traditional rhyme with the group.

*"Five little ducks went swimming one
    day,
Over the hills and far away.
Mother Duck said, 'Quack, quack, quack,
    quack.'
But only four little ducks came back."*

## Poetic language tickles the tongue, tingles the mind, and intrigues the ear.

**Poetry and verse as predictable texts are easy to read.** They contain short lines with few words per line, rhyming words, melody, few words that say a great deal, much white space with few words on a page, and the natural language of childhood.

**Poetry helps children learn to listen.** Children pay attention to poetry because it accentuates the sounds of language—for example, *"An earthworm doesn't make a sound / When he's working underground."* (Ernesto Galarza); *"Caterpillars crawl humpity-hump / Little frogs go jumpity-jump.";* and *"Always quiet, / Always blinking, / By day sleeping, / At night winking."* (Nelly Palacio Jaramillo)

**Poetry teaches children new vocabulary.** Poetry uses interesting words in interesting ways. Children notice new words and repeat them in their conversations.

**Poetry helps children learn to read.** Beginning readers learn to decode print in poetry because the lines are short, the words rhyme, and the accent falls on meaningful words. These clues tell readers what is coming next—for example,

> *"Elephant,*
> *Elephant,*
> *Big as a House!*
> *They tell me*
> *That you*
> *Are afraid of a*
> *Mouse."* (Langston Hughes)

**Poetry helps children make connections between letters and sounds**. Children learn phonics when they see patterns of letters and sounds repeated in poetry and verse. Poetry helps reluctant or disabled readers because there are not many words on a page. Poems leave much white space—open space—on a page. The short lines and limited number of words do not intimidate a child learning to read—for example, *"Good books. / Good times. / Good stories. / Good rhymes."* (Lee Bennett Hopkins)

**Poetry helps children learn to write.** Children learn to read by writing; poetry lets them in on the secret of how words work. They discover that if they can write *my hat*, they can also write *my cat* and *my bat*. When they learn to write *quack*, they can also write *shack, snack, tack, track,* and *backpack*. These discoveries turn struggling writers into wordsmiths—for example, *"Send in the Cat / to chase that Rat! / Send*
*in the Hog / to shoo that Dog! / Send in the Cow. / Send that Cow NOW!"* (Wong Herbert Yee)

**Poetry helps children learn to think.** It shows them new images and new ways to view the world—for example, *"A dream is just a pillow away."* (from "How Far" by Leland B. Jacobs in *Big Book of Rhymes*); *"I've also proved by actual test, / A wet dog is the lovingest."* (Ogden Nash); and *"A soft dog, / A furry dog, / A call-her-and-she'll-hurry dog."* (Nancy Klima)

## Strategies for the Classroom

Copy poems onto large chart paper and laminate for durability. Use the charts to read together and to point out similarities in word patterns, initial consonants, and other phonics elements.

Read the same poems over and over until children know them by heart. Present a program for other class groups or for parents to demonstrate children's wealth of poetic knowledge.

Create a display that includes poems children love and poems children write. On a table, bulletin board, or wall, display poems children have brought in, written, or copied from books. 🍎

---

### BOOKLIST

*Eek! There's a Mouse in the House,* by Wong Herbert Yee, Houghton Mifflin, 1992.

*The Llama Who Had No Pajama: 100 Favorite Poems,* by Mary Ann Hoberman, Harcourt Brace & Co., 1998.

*Kids Pick the Funniest Poems,* compiled by Bruce Lansky, Meadowbrook Press, 1991.

*How Now Brown Cow?* by Alice Schertie, Harcourt Brace & Co., 1998.

*The Sweet and Sour Animal Book,* by Langston Hughes, Oxford University Press, 1994.

# WHEN A FEATHER FALLS:

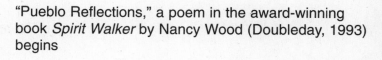
## using poetry with children

by Dr. Lee Bennett Hopkins
Poet, Author, Anthologist

"Pueblo Reflections," a poem in the award-winning book *Spirit Walker* by Nancy Wood (Doubleday, 1993) begins

> "When a feather falls at your feet,
> it means you are to travel
> on wings of curiosity."

When I started my career as an elementary school teacher in 1960, the feather that fell at my feet was one that quivered with poetry. I quickly realized how poetry could change and enhance the lives of my children, how it could stir their emotions with a minimum of words and lines like no other form of literature. Via poetry, my children and I could laugh and cry, sing and shout, be totally surprised and awed at what poetry could give us.

Throughout my entire professional life, I have continued to use poetry with children on every grade level, at every age, from preschoolers through college-schoolers!

Let the feather fall at your feet, and your teaching life will be enhanced, too.

## Use Poetry Every Day In Every Area of the Curriculum

Try using poetry with math, science, and social studies—as well as language arts.

## Think About Combining Other Works of Fiction and Nonfiction With Poetry, No Matter What the Topic Is.

You will find there are poems written on almost any subject—from fingerprints to wildflowers, secrets to seals, dreamers to dancers. Anthologies can provide a wealth of complementary selections centered around powerful themes and topics. Many such groupings can help you connect literature to science, social studies, and math.

## Start Students on a Search For Poetry.

If your students enjoy a particular poet's work, encourage them to seek out individual collections or verses the poet has written that appear in anthologies. Chances are, if students delight in a poem by John Ciardi, Eve Merriam, or Nikki Giovanni, for example, they will appreciate other offerings by the same poets.

Once poetry becomes a part of students' repertoires, class projects might center around choosing

- "The Poem of the Week,"
- "The Poet of the Month," or
- "Best Poems About ___"
  —any topic of the students' choice.

**When the feather falls at your feet, pick it up.** See how quickly you and your students will "travel on wings of curiosity." I *know* you will.

**Happy journeying!**

# BOOKLIST

## TEACHER RESOURCES

**Pass the Poetry, Please!** by Lee Bennett Hopkins, 3rd ed. HarperCollins Publishers. 1998. Describes methods by which a teacher may introduce children to the appreciation and creation of poetry.

**Using Poetry Across the Curriculum: A Whole Language Approach** by Barbara Chatton. Oryx Press, 1993. Offers elementary school teachers a formula for integrating poetry into all areas of study by exploiting their interconnections.

**Let's Do a Poem: Introducing Poetry to Children** by Nancy Larrick. Delacorte, 1991. Introduces poetry to children through listening, singing, chanting, impromptu choral reading, body movement, dance, and dramatization.

## BOOKS FOR CHILDREN

**A Lucky Thing** by Alice Schertle. San Diego: Harcourt Brace & Co. 1999. A collection of poems about nature.

**Beast Feast: Poems and Paintings** by Douglas Florian. Spoken Arts. 1998. A collection on videocassette of humorous poems about such animals as the walrus, anteater, and boa.

**Bing Bang Boing: Poems and Drawings** by Douglas, Florian. Puffin Books. 1996. An illustrated collection of more than 150 nonsense verses.

**Gracie Graves and the Kids from Room 402** by Betty Paraskevas. Harcourt Brace & Co. 1995. Brief humorous poems describe each of the fourteen boys and thirteen girls in Ms. Gracie Graves' class.

**Insectlopedia: Poems and Painting** by Douglas Florian. Scholastic. 1999. Twenty-one short poems about such insects as the inchworm, termite, cricket, and ladybug.

**Laugh-eteria: Poems and Drawings** by Douglas Florian. Harcourt Brace & Co. 1999. 100 humorous poems on such topics as ogres, pizza, fear, school, dragons, trees, and hair.

**The Llama Who Had No Pajama: 100 favorite poems.** Harcourt Brace & Co. 1998. An illustrated collection of poems about all sorts of subjects.

**The Random House Book of Poetry for Children** Ed. by Jack Prelutsky. Random House, 1983. More than 550 poems included.

# USING FICTION AND INFORMATIONAL BOOKS:
# grOwIng
## WITH THE GRAIN

**by Dr. Bernice E. Cullinan**
Professor of Early Childhood
and Elementary Education,
New York University

I grew up on a farm and find that I sprinkle my writing repeatedly with images of planting, growing, cultivating, and nurturing. I believe that seeds planted early take deep root; I want the seeds of literacy to be planted deeply and early. The American writer, Willa Cather, said that our writing grows from the land beneath our feet. Images I use show this to be true.

Students who spread their wings as readers discover a wealth of books to support their flight. A developmental reading and language arts program serves as a launching pad to introduce students to the very best writers in the widest variety of genres. Students strike out on their own to read numerous informational books, fictional stories about real or make-believe people, and poetry that makes them laugh and cry. Teachers use an integrated response-centered curriculum to probe the wealth of resources on every topic.

# strategies

## Library Research on Food

Ask students to explore library resources in section 633.1 to learn about corn, wheat, rice, and other cereal grains. Let students use an encyclopedia on CD-ROM to watch mushrooms growing, yeast rising, wheat being threshed, and food being processed.

## Read About Grains

Have students read recipes for grain foods, such as baked barley and peanut casserole, rice and beans, cornbread, wheat cakes, and muffins. Students can choose recipes to prepare and sample.

## Geography and Food

Every country has its native bread and basic food staple. Ask students to match each type of bread with its country of origin on a map of the world. Have them post a symbol of the type of bread—such as pita bread, seven-grain bread, bagels, pizza, matzoh, baking soda biscuits, cornbread, pancakes, yeast rolls, and wheat bread—on the country. Then ask students to identify the country of origin for basic grain dishes, such as couscous, polenta, kasha, rice, corn, wheat, oatmeal, beans and rice, barley, peanuts, legumes, beans, and peas. (Read from *A Chorus of Cultures* by Alma Flor Ada.)

## Food, Language, and Literature

Food is referred to in slang, idioms, sayings, and proverbs. Have students collect sayings about food, such as "Two peas in a pod," "Use your bean," "Half a loaf is better than none," "Don't go against the grain." References to food and grain appear in poetic language, such as "walking in fields of gold" and "separate the wheat from the chaff," and in song and poetry, such as "Jimmy crack corn," "Timothy Tompkins had turnips for tea," "You'll remember me when the west wind moves upon the fields of barley," and "Don't sit under the apple tree." References to food appear in folklore, such as *The Turnip: A Russian Tale*, retold by Pleasant DeSpain, and *The Lotus Seed*, retold by Sherry Garland. Ask students to search for language about food as they read.

# FOR THE CLASSROOM

## Writing, Food, and Me

Encourage students to write "All About Me" booklets. Topics might include "When I Wake Up," "Snacks I Like," and "What I Like for Dinner." Ask students to keep a food diary for a week and to write about their favorite foods. Then have them write poems about eating food, such as slurping spaghetti, sipping soup, and popping popcorn. Encourage students to read Arnold Adoff's *Eats* and learn why Adoff is called the "popcorn poet."

## Changing Fashions in Food

Ask students to survey parents, the school's nutritionists, and other knowledgeable people to find out about dietary changes and about foods that are considered healthful. Have students make graphs of responses showing how many people eat various foods. Then ask students to compare a fast-food menu with a home-cooked menu for food value and cost factors. (Read "Think Positive" from *Current Health*, April 1993, pp. 30–31.)

## Math and Food

Have students read consumer education and ecology magazines, such as *Zillions: Consumer Reports for Kids*, *Kids for Saving Earth News*, and *National Geographic World*. Then ask them to measure quantities for recipes, determine cost per pound of various grains, and price-shop at a local supermarket to determine how much basic foods cost.

## Nature, Food, and Creatures

The area surrounding a tree feeds many different kinds of creatures. Ask students to read *The Great Kapok Tree*, by Lynne Cherry, and list all the creatures that live in, on, under, or near the Kapok tree. Have students read about tropical rain forests and locate all the creatures that live there.

## Animals and Food

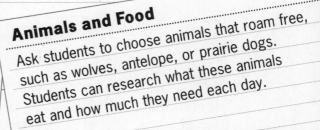

Ask students to choose animals that roam free, such as wolves, antelope, or prairie dogs. Students can research what these animals eat and how much they need each day.

## Science, Food, and Nature

Discuss with students the interdependence among animals, grasslands, oceans, and people. Encourage students to create graphics or displays that illustrate food chains and interdependence.

# Guidelines for Choosing Multicultural Literature

by Dr. Junko Yokota—*Associate Professor, National College of Education, National-Louis University, Evanston, Illinois*

The role of multicultural literature in the classroom is to provide all students with extensive opportunities to learn about the contributions, achievements, and traditions of people from diverse groups, to see their own culture depicted in literature, and to develop accurate concepts of self, others, and the world around us.

Literature forms the basis of a truly integrated reading and language arts program. Using *multicultural* literature simply means that children benefit from a rich variety of the best authors, illustrators, characters, and real-life heroes. Here are some guidelines to keep in mind when selecting multicultural literature:

- Include a **variety of genres:** folklore, poetry, historical fiction, informational articles, realistic fiction, biography and autobiography, fantasy, and mystery.
- Select literature that is written and illustrated by someone who holds an **"insider's" perspective** of the culture portrayed.
- Check for **cultural accuracy,** both in the overall treatment of various issues and in the details. (Tip: If you are not sure of the accuracy yourself, ask colleagues and other community members for advice.)
- Try to find literature that is **culturally specific:** a story about Korean Americans rather than Asian Americans or about a Sioux family rather than a Native American family.
- Include literature about ethnic groups in the **United States,** both present and past, suburban, urban, and rural.
- Include literature with settings in other countries.
- Depict **differing perspectives** to show multidimensionality within groups; recognize that there are many differences within as well as between various ethnic and cultural groups.

**This chart shows one way of thinking about multicultural understanding. If your students can perform on all three of these levels, you will know that you have helped them appreciate diversity.**

## Multicultural Literature

### Achievement Level
Students are aware of the contributions of all groups and cultures in art, science, literature, and other areas.

### Diverse Perspectives Level
Students are able to see events and ideas from the viewpoints of people with various backgrounds.

### Decision-Making Level
Students draw on their understanding of achievements and perspectives of diverse groups as they make decisions and judgments.

### Levels of Understanding

# LITERATURE CIRCLES

BY DR. JUDY WALLIS
K–12 COORDINATOR
SPRING BRANCH
INDEPENDENT
SCHOOL DISTRICT,
HOUSTON, TEXAS

Groups of students gather with their books in hand. Small journals are tucked neatly inside their books. Within a few moments, the five groups of students seated around the room initiate discussion. One group's conversation about *Sarah, Plain and Tall*, by Patricia MacLachlan, follows:

**Thom:** I don't think Sarah really understood how hard it was for Caleb and Anna to accept a new mother.

**Keesha:** Why do you say that? Sarah didn't expect them to love her right away. I think she was waiting for them to feel okay about her being there. I felt sorry for Sarah.

**Fernando:** Well, I really liked this book. My favorite part was this. (He points to a page marked with a self-stick note.) It just made me feel happy when she wrote "Tell them I sing." I thought she seemed funny but nice.

**Justin:** I have an uncle like that. He cracks people up, but he's really nice, too.

Thom suggests that they take out their journals. The small journals are made of four or five sheets of plain paper folded and stapled. The students have written the title of their book and the author's name on the front cover. Inside, they have jotted thoughts about the text, reflections about themselves as readers, and responses to prompts like the following:

*The story was interesting because ...*
*My favorite character was ... because ...*
*The ending of the story made me feel ...*

A lively discussion follows, and students explore the text further.

Louise Rosenblatt (1978) introduced the idea of aesthetic and efferent reading stances. She suggested that much of the reading done in school centers around what students "carry away" from the reading experience. Too little attention, she contended, is given to the transaction that occurs between reader and text. The literary experience is not simply the result of comprehending the text;

it is the personal connections that make reading memorable.

Literature circles, also known as book clubs or response groups, are arranged around choices of texts and membership and are growing in popularity. Teachers have discovered that when they provide supportive environments and model thoughtful responses, students offer multiple interpretations and complex understandings. The quality of discussion and the appreciation of literature matures as students are given opportunities to explore texts as well as their peers' unique perspectives.

A crucial phase of the literary experience comes when students sharpen their interpretations by considering the theme in the context of real life. In the students' discussion of *Sarah, Plain and Tall,* they saw Sarah's relationship to Caleb and Anna through their personal experiences. Their differences gave opportunities to analyze, explain, and defend their own responses. As students conclude such a discussion, they can be assisted in summarizing their own understandings and in considering topics for future discussions.

Let's rejoin the group . . .

| Fernando: | I wonder what will happen to Anna and Caleb. |
|---|---|
| Keesha: | I think they will live happily ever after. |
| Justin: | Yeah, but they will always miss their mom, just like Wilbur missed Charlotte in *Charlotte's Web.* |

Students begin book studies with their own perceptions. However, they soon learn that exploring others' ideas and thinking about multiple interpretations of texts can lead to rich and meaningful reading experiences.

# Tips for Starting Literature Circles

- Read aloud each day; pick 3–4 books to study as a class.

- Invite students to share favorite authors and illustrators.

- Work with students to establish guidelines that include
  — how to listen to others,
  — how to contribute to the discussion,
  — taking turns,
  — respecting others' opinions.

- Decide how books and group members will be selected. (Students can make more of the choices themselves as time goes on.)

- Use a variety of response activities, for example:
  — logs and journals
  — story maps and other graphics
  — art projects
  — character studies
  — storytelling

- Enjoy!

© Harcourt

# OFTEN-ASKED QUESTIONS ABOUT
# Vocabulary Development

by Dr. W. Dorsey Hammond, Professor of Education, Oakland University, Rochester, Michigan

**Q How important is vocabulary instruction in an integrated language arts curriculum?**

**A** Vocabulary instruction is very important. However, we need to look at vocabulary in a broader context. We should think of vocabulary in terms of language development. People with a good vocabulary don't just know the meanings of many words; they have versatility with language. They use the right word for the right occasion. They have *variety* and *flexibility* in language and word usage. That is why vocabulary is best developed in the context of literature and all the language arts.

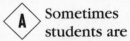

**Q Students often seem unmotivated by vocabulary activities. Why?**

**A** Sometimes students are bored because they see no reason for the vocabulary activities they are doing. The activities are separated from the stories they are reading and writing. Or sometimes students are required to look up lists of words in dictionaries and write the words in sentences. Some students are asked to memorize definitions. These activities simply don't work and students tend to understand that.

**Q How can we improve our students' vocabulary and language?**

**A** We should begin with a basic truth: Children and adults who read a great deal tend to have good vocabularies. The best way to improve vocabulary is to have a strong reading and writing curriculum. It is true, of course, that we need vocabulary in order to read; it is also very true that as we read we increase our vocabulary and versatility with language.

**Q Can vocabulary be developed through direct instruction?**

**A** Yes, as long as it's taught in a meaningful context.

**Q Can you give an example of teaching vocabulary in a meaningful context?**

**A** After children finish reading a story, ask them to pick out two or three words or phrases that they found the most interesting, and discuss them.

Assume that your students have just completed "The Midnight Fox" by Betsy Byars. After the reading, you might refer to the following passage:

The baby fox did not move for a moment. I could barely see him . . . He waited, alert and suspicious, and then after a moment he moved in a crouch to the door of the cage.

© Harcourt

Ask students to describe what is happening in this passage: "What does it mean to be *alert* and *suspicious*?" Ask students to role-play this behavior. Talk about the word *moment*. "How long is that? How is *moment* a better word than *instant*?" "What does it mean to *crouch*? Show us." "Betsy Byars wrote, *I could barely see him.* What other word could she have used in place of *barely*? Yes, *hardly*."

In this example we are sensitizing students to how an author uses words to paint a picture in the reader's mind. Another strategy is to ask students after reading to choose two or three words or phrases that they found most interesting or that were new to them. Encourage discussion.

**Q Are you saying that the best time to develop vocabulary is after the reading?**

**A** In most cases, yes. Then it is meaningful and in context. As students respond to a story, they can talk about interesting language, new words, old words with new meanings, and so on.

**Q Don't children need to know the meanings of all the words in order to understand a story?**

**A** They need to know the meanings of most words—but not all. To decide which words to teach students before reading a text story, use the following key. If condition 1 prevails, teach the word or phrase *before* reading and review it after reading. If condition 2, 3, or 4 prevails, it is probably best to address these words and phrases *after* reading.

1. The word (or phrase) is essential for comprehension and not defined in context.

2. The word is essential but is defined in context.

3. The word is not necessary for adequate comprehension.

4. The word is not necessary but is interesting.

**Q Can you give examples of words defined in context?**

**A** Sure. Look at the following sentences: "Imagine a line of a thousand camels, one after the other, carrying salt, silk, and tea across the desert. Such caravans . . ." Notice that we are given the definition and then the label. And here is another example: "The castle is surrounded by a water-filled ditch called a moat." In this example, we have an explicit definition of *moat*.

The important issue here is that we discuss this context strategy with our students. We need to teach students not only *about* language but *how* language works in authentic texts.

**Q Do you have a favorite activity for vocabulary development?**

**A** I like the mapping or webbing of words. You begin with a word, describe its higher-order class, list its properties, and give examples. here is a map of the word *computer*:

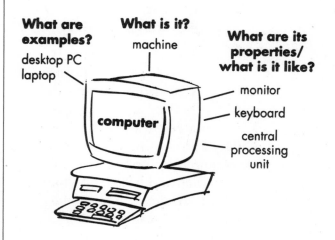

You can do this map with any noun and even with many verbs and adverbs. You could try it with such words as *school, crouch, suspicious, moat,* or *caravan,* for example. Working in pairs, students seem to enjoy doing vocabulary maps of words they are interested in.

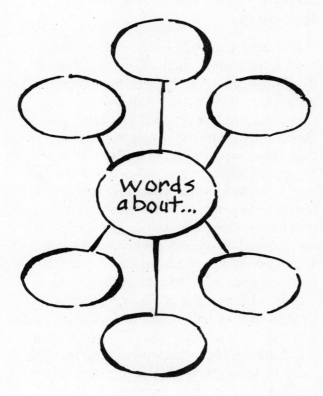

Some basic guidelines for developing vocabulary:

✔ Talk about words—interesting words, unusual words, new words, or old words with new meanings.

✔ Teach in context whenever possible.

✔ Teach students how to use context to figure out new words.

✔ Focus on just a few words at a time. It is better to learn three words well than to learn ten words superficially.

✔ Promote words. Maintain a wall chart with the three or four most interesting words students have read or heard this week.

✔ Think in terms of phrases and sentences and interesting sayings.

✔ Use literature as a model of how words can be used. Good authors are masters at choosing just the right word.

✔ Promote variety and versatility. Talk about how even a simple word can have many shades of meanings; for example, *hit* the ball, a *hit* show, *hit* the nail on the head, *hit* and run, *hit* the deck, and so on.

✔ Compliment students when they use interesting language in their conversation and writing.

✔ Remember that words aren't just learned or not learned. There are degrees of learning. Some words we understand in depth. Other words we have an average understanding of. Then there are words we "sort of" know the meanings of, but can't really explain. Vocabulary and language growth is an ongoing process for both children and adults.

# FREE READING *and* VOCABULARY

## by Stephen Krashen, Ph.D.
### Professor, Curriculum and Teaching, University of Southern California

**Thanks to research done largely in the last few years, there is now overwhelming evidence that reading is the best way to build vocabulary.**

## More Reading Results in Larger Vocabularies for Readers

Students who participate in school-based reading programs, such as Sustained Silent Reading, make greater gains on standardized vocabulary tests, while students who say they read additional books and other materials on their own have larger vocabularies than those who don't (Krashen, 1989). Moreover, readers themselves know the benefits of reading. Smith and Supanich (1984) tested 456 company presidents and reported that they had significantly larger vocabularies than did a comparison group of adults. When asked if they had made an effort to increase their vocabularies since leaving school, 54.5 percent of the company presidents said they had. When those respondents were asked what they did to increase their vocabularies, about half mentioned reading. Only 14 subjects (6 percent of those who tried to increase their vocabularies) mentioned vocabulary instruction books.

Laboratory studies confirm that vocabulary knowledge can be acquired through reading. In these studies, subjects are asked to read a passage containing unfamiliar words. After reading the passage, they are tested on the words. These studies show that when an unfamiliar word is seen in print, "a small but statistically reliable increase in word knowledge" typically occurs (Nagy, Herman, and Anderson, 1985). These results hold for both first-language and second-language readers (Krashen, 1993; Pitss, White, and Krashen, 1989; Day, Omura, and Hiramatsu, 1991; Dupuy and Krashen, 1993).

Listening to stories also builds vocabulary. Preschool children who have heard more stories than their peers go on to have larger vocabularies at age ten (Wells, 1986), and children's vocabulary knowledge grows when they hear stories containing unfamiliar words (Eller, Pappas, and Brown, 1988; Elley, 1989).

## The Limits of Direct Instruction of Vocabulary

The usual means of acquiring new vocabulary in school are drills and exercises. The effectiveness of direct vocabulary instruction, however, is severely limited. One reason for this is that there are simply too many words for students to learn at one time. Estimates of adult vocabulary size range from 40,000 to 150,000 (Krashen, 1993). (A few recent studies have claimed that adults know fewer words, about 17,000—but these studies restricted possible vocabulary size by excluding many kinds of words; see Krashen, 1992, for discussion.) In addition, it has been estimated that schoolchildren between the grades of three and twelve learn 3,000 new words per year. No vocabulary teaching program can come close to this learning rate. Vocabulary must come from somewhere else.

The results of the laboratory studies mentioned earlier strongly suggest that reading alone is enough to support reported rates of acquisition. Nagy et al., for example, estimate that each time we see a word in print, we get about five to ten percent of its meaning. Furthermore, we can assume that

> But what should students read about, listen to, write about, and discuss? A good literature program supplies the answer: ideas. Students read and hear stories that encourage them to reflect on their lives, they discuss and occasionally debate these ideas, and they write about the ideas.

about one million words per year is an average amount of reading for middle-class students (Anderson, Wilson, and Fielding, 1988). Nagy et al. conclude that just this small increment in word knowledge is enough to account for annual vocabulary growth. In other words, reading can do the job of teaching word knowledge.

A million words is not a huge amount of reading. Typically, comic books contain about 2,000 words, while teen romances often contain 40,000 to 50,000 words. Some students, according to Anderson, Wilson, and Fielding (1988), are reading a lot more than a million words per year. They are reading 2 million, 5 million, or even 10 million words per year. Clearly, students with larger vocabularies are not doing more drills and exercises; they are reading more.

Learning words through reading is ten times as efficient, in terms of words acquired per minute, as drills and exercises (Nagy, Herman, and Anderson, 1985). Reading is ten times as effective—and at least a hundred times more interesting—than vocabulary drill, and we learn many things from reading besides vocabulary.

In my view, the best kind of reading for developing vocabulary is voluntary reading. There is good evidence that when students read what they want to read, they do not simply choose easy books; rather, they choose books that are interesting (Krashen, 1995). There are, of course, great advantages to having all students in a group read and discuss the same test, and there will be times when an unfamiliar but crucial word should be explained by the teacher. Such explanations may help students learn a *few* words. But most of their vocabulary will be acquired via wide-ranging, self-selected reading.

## Cause and Effect

It is crucial to understand that linguistic and cognitive development are results of students' "wrestling with" ideas–reading about them, listening to them, writing about them, and discussing them. We don't first learn language and facts and then apply them in the study of literature. Literature is the source of linguistic and cognitive development. If students and teachers focus on the ideas in literature, on the stories and their meanings, linguistic and cognitive development will occur as a natural outcome.

## Free Voluntary Reading

An indirect but very powerful payoff of participating in a literature program is that well-taught literature programs instill in students a love of books and a desire to read on their own. Because free reading makes such a large contribution to the development of literacy, one can even claim that a successful literature program is one in which students are reading more independently.

## What About Literature in the First Language?

Studying literature in a student's first language is not a luxury. There is good reason to believe it will help the student acquire English more rapidly and provide him or her with the knowledge and abilities necessary for success in the English-speaking mainstream. A good literature program in the primary language offers these advantages:

- *Background knowledge*   Students who study literature in their primary language gain knowledge of the world as well as an understanding of what literature is. Good books and helpful, teacher-guided discussion can inform students about social studies and science. This knowledge helps make English input on these subjects more comprehensible and thus accelerates English-language development. In addition, a student who participates in a good literature program in the primary language learns how to discuss and write about the ideas in a story and also develops an appreciation of good literature. This foundation makes the study of literature in English more comprehensible and more meaningful.

- *Literacy transfers*   As noted earlier, developing literacy in one language facilitates the development of literacy in another. In addition, there is every reason to hypothesize that those who read for pleasure in one language will also read for pleasure in another language.

# The Synchrony of Reading and Spelling Development:
## HOW CHILDREN LEARN ABOUT WORDS

by Dr. Donald R. Bear

Dr. Bear is Professor and Director of Curriculum and Instruction at the College of Education, University of Nevada, Reno.

### OLD MISTER RABBIT

#### *D. Lipman*

1. Old Mister Rabbit,
You've got a mighty habit,
Of jumping in my garden
And eating all my cabbage.

2. Old Mister Rabbit,
You've got a mighty habit,
Of jumping in my garden
And eating all my broccoli.

3. Old Mister Rabbit,
You've got a mighty habit,
Of jumping in my garden
And eating all my tomatoes.

4. Old Mister Rabbit,
You've got a mighty habit,
Of jumping in my garden
And eating all my ice cream.

If you were to choral read "Old Mister Rabbit" a few times with your children and then ask individuals to try to read it independently, could you predict which of them would be able to? Children in the emergent stage of literacy could do a fair job *approximating* the text, based on their familiarity with it.

Children who cannot reliably track text by pointing with a finger as they read would have particular difficulty tracking two-syllable words. For example, in the phrase *Old Mister Rabbit*, they might say /tur/ when pointing to *Rabbit*, thinking it was the second syllable in *Mister*. A child's ability to track print tells a lot about his or her concept of word (Morris, 1981). Not surprisingly, it also helps us identify his or her stage of spelling development.

**Figure 1. Synchrony of Literacy Development**

**Reading Stages and Behaviors**

| Emergent | Beginning | | Transitional |
|---|---|---|---|
| No concept of word<br>Pretend reading | Rudimentary concept<br>of word<br>Reads with support<br>Disfluent and<br>unexpressive reading<br>Finger-point reading<br>Reads aloud to self | Functional concept<br>of word<br>Reads longer passages<br>with support | Approaching fluency<br>Reads easy chapter<br>books |

**Stages of Spelling and Word Study Activities**

| Preliterate Stage | Early Letter-Name Stage | Letter-Name Stage | Within-Word-Pattern Stage |
|---|---|---|---|
| Examples<br>Scribbles | B or BD for *bed*<br>D, J, G, JR, or DRV<br>for *drive*<br>F, FL, or FLT for *float* | BAD for *bed*<br>JRIV, DIV, or DRIV for<br>*drive*<br>FOT or FLOT for *float* | Spells *bed* correctly<br>DRIEV or spells *drive*<br>correctly<br>FLOTE or spells *float*<br>correctly |
| Activities<br>Concept sort<br>Alphabet songs<br>Alphabet games | Collect words for<br>Word Bank; sort<br>pictures for initial<br>consonants; some<br>analysis of final<br>consonants; some<br>analysis of consonant<br>blends and digraphs | Study word families;<br>study short vowels<br>with picture and<br>word sorts | Word sorts; word study<br>notebooks; study<br>long vowel patterns;<br>*r*-controlled vowels;<br>other vowel patterns |

(based on Henderson, 1990, and adapted from Bear, 1991)

## Emergent Readers and Preliterate Spelling

Children who cannot match written text with what they are saying are in the "preliterate" stage of spelling. This means that when they write, they use a blend of squiggles and recognizable letter forms that lacks a consistent sound-symbol correspondence between what they wrote and what they *say* they wrote.

### Word Study: Preliterate Stage

Children's word study at this stage consists of such activities as learning the letter names of the alphabet, singing the alphabet song, matching uppercase and lowercase letters, and categorizing words and objects. Children do not learn many sight words until the next stage of development.

## Beginning Readers and Early Letter-Name Spelling

Once children have acquired a rudimentary concept of word, they begin to collect a sight vocabulary. They can read a poem such as "Old Mister Rabbit" with some accuracy, in part because they are better at tracking print. These children are called beginning readers.

As shown in Figure 1, throughout this stage you will see the following reading behaviors:

- Children read aloud when they read to themselves.
- Children point to the words as they read.
- Children tend to read disfluently (Bear, 1989).

Given the synchrony of reading and spelling development, we can predict that these children are probably in either the "Early Letter-Name" or "Letter-Name" stage of spelling.

Early Letter-Name spellers usually choose logical beginning and final consonants for the sounds in the words they are trying to spell (Figure 1). Some spellings are based on how the words "feel" in their mouths when they say them (Read, 1975). Using this strategy, children in the Early Letter-Name stage often spell *dr* as *JR*. If you try saying these two digraphs yourself, you'll realize that this is a logical invention. The sounds /dr/ and /jr/ are articulated in nearly the same way. Also, children at this stage often omit vowels in their writing, except in important words like their own names.

## *Word Study:* Early Letter-Name Stage

Children can sort their sight words by initial consonants. They enjoy hunting through familiar texts for words that begin with the same sound they are studying.

# Beginning Readers and Letter-Name Spelling

In the early stages of beginning reading, children have a rudimentary concept of word. That is, if you ask them to find a particular word, they need to go back to the beginning of a line or to the beginning of the rhyme to find it. Children in the later stages of beginning reading are able to find the word without going back.

The difference in spelling between these two groups is quite remarkable. Children with a functional concept of word have progressed to the Letter-Name stage of spelling. This means that they continue to use a letter-name strategy to spell, but vowels have been added. Often they try to spell short vowel sounds based on the way the vowels feel in the mouth. For example, some children spell the short *e* in *bed* with the letter name *a* because the *a* feels that way in their mouths when they say it.

Children in the Letter-Name stage can sort known words based on the sound in the middle of the word. At first, children look at the similarities within families (*fat,*

*cat, bat, rat*). After examining other short-vowel families, children begin to see the consonant-vowel-consonant (CVC) pattern. These children can generalize that the vowels in *cat, fan,* and even *ball* are all short *a*'s.

## *Word Study:* Letter-Name Stage

Children are ready to learn about short-vowel families and the basic short-vowel patterns. However, long-vowel patterns should not be introduced because these spellers continue to use a single vowel to spell long vowels, for example, *cot* for *coat*.

# Transitional Readers and Within-Word-Pattern Spelling

Toward the end of first grade, many children move to the next stage of literacy development. This is a transitional period in which children begin reading silently and generally need less support than beginning readers. Predictable text becomes less important, and as noted in the chart, easy chapter books are often chosen.

Given the synchrony of development, we see that transitional readers are in the Within-Word-Pattern stage of spelling (Bear, 1992). During this stage, children have learned to spell most short-vowel words and CVC patterns, and their invented spellings show them to be experimenting with long-vowel spelling patterns. They know enough about long- and short-vowel patterns to know that the word *coat* cannot be spelled *cot*, and they begin to use long-vowel patterns as they spell.

## *Word Study:* Transitional Stage

Children examine long-vowel patterns for differences and similarities. They spend some time studying one vowel and its various patterns; for example, the CVVC pattern in *nail* and the CVCe pattern in *name*.

© Harcourt

# Strategies for Studying Words

Dr. Robert Schlagal

Associate Professor, Reich College of Education, Appalachian State University, Boone, North Carolina

▼ ▼ ▼ ▼ ▼ ▼ ▼ ▼ ▼ ▼ ▼ ▼ ▼ ▼ ▼ ▼ ▼ ▼

The third, fourth, and fifth grades comprise a potentially rich and productive period for the growth of children's knowledge of English spelling. Broadly speaking, children in this period (1) solidify and broaden their command of vowel patterns in one-syllable words. From this base, they (2) learn the conventions of marking short and long vowels across syllables—the consonant doubling and *e*-drop conventions—and how these principles apply in polysyllabic words (*rabbit* vs. *basic*). Furthermore, (3) they become acquainted with the meaning principle in spelling, first through homophones and later with derivational pairs (e.g., *sign-signal, reduce-reduction*). And (4) children learn to pay attention to stress patterns in polysyllabic words as a means to identify "hard spots" in words.

## Steps to Spelling Success

There are four critical steps in helping children develop their word knowledge efficiently and permanently:

1. The first step is the regular study of lists of words organized around developmentally appropriate patterns. (This is most efficiently done through well-developed spelling instruction.)

2. The next step is making sure that children are studying words at an appropriate level of difficulty. (Judgments of this kind can be made by giving a periodic review as a diagnostic tool for future word study.)

3. The third step involves helping children to study specific groups of words by sound and pattern. (Such activities help

students to see, retain, and generalize patterns they are studying.)

4. The last step is to involve children in frequent, purposeful writing activities in which they can express their growing command of written English in natural ways.

I will focus my attention here on informal word study activities which teachers can use to heighten the impact of their spelling instruction. One appropriate time to use these activities is during the editing or proofreading stage of the writing process, whenever one or more students show difficulty with a particular spelling pattern.

## Word Study Activities

Teacher-guided **word sorts** are a very effective way of helping children see and use order in English spelling. Word sorting is a comparison/contrast activity in which children physically group words together by sound and pattern in order to highlight word structure and promote its automatic recognition. Let's take an example from the kind of patterns third-grade children may be expected to master.

By third grade, most children have gained control of basic short vowel patterns and consonant blends. Long vowels, however, are not so easily mastered, for they are spelled in a variety of ways. Third-graders are aware of many of these varied patterns but often use them unreliably. The word *soap* or *chase*, for instance, might be spelled SOPE or CHAISE. Basic word-sorting tasks can be used to help children gain control of these patterns. One way to set this up would be as follows:

The teacher has a pocket chart fixed to the wall of the classroom. She decides that a group of four or five students would benefit from work with varied long *o* patterns. Her object is to provide practice with long *o* words, specifically the *oe, o_e, ow,* and *oa* patterns. Using index cards, she prints four or five examples of each pattern, each on a separate card.

The teacher calls over the group of children and explains that they are going to do an activity with some long *o* words. (She may wish to use a more elaborate explanation, but this is not necessary.) She then places one card for each category across the top of the pocket chart like this:

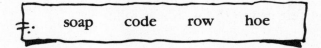

| soap | code | row | hoe |

Then she holds up a new card, the word *loan,* for instance, and asks, "What's this word? Right, Marie. I'm going to put *loan* under the word *soap.* (She fits it into the pocket chart directly below *soap.*)

"Okay, José, what's this one?" The teacher holds up the word *bone.* (Note: It is important that the words used in the sort be known words. Words that can't be identified by the group should be put aside.) "Good, José, will you come up and put *bone* where you think it should go?" José takes the card and hesitates for a few moments but places it under the word *code.* "Okay, what do the rest of you think? Do you agree with José's decision?" (Checking out each word placement with the group is helpful in several ways. First, it keeps the other students engaged when it is not their turn. Second, it focuses the students on each of the words—not just their own—in relation to the target patterns. And, third, if an error is made, the group and not the teacher helps correct it.) At the end of this sort, the pocket chart might look like this:

| soap | code | row | hoe |
| loan | bone | know | toe |
| float | hope | flow | woe |
| boat | rope | blow | doe |

Once the sort is complete, the teacher may ask the group to figure out how the words in a given column are alike. This helps students identify the pattern that they saw and used to make the sort.

To reinforce pattern recognition, the teacher can play a game of **concentration.** This is done by mixing up the cards and turning them face down on the pocket chart. Each child gets a chance to come up and turn over two cards. If a child gets a match (two words that fit a single pattern), she holds on to them and takes another turn. If the pair of cards do not match, she sits down and the next child takes a turn.

This sort should be repeated until the individuals in the group can sort smoothly, accurately, and quickly. The object here is not simply accuracy of decision-making, but fluency.

To highlight a basic syllable-juncture operation, a **two-column sort** can be used. A short *a* versus long *a* comparison/contrast sort (adding *-ed* or *-ing*) might look something like this:

| clapping | taking |
| tapped | facing |
| chatted | blamed |
| grabbing | traded |
| planning | faked |
| snapped | baking |

(Note: In this sort, each time a student sorts a word into a column, she can be asked to spell the base word. In that case, if Jennie correctly placed *blamed* under the column headed by *taking,* she would say "blame,

b-l-a-m-e." This helps heighten awareness of the relationship between the pattern of the base word and its inflected form.)

To increase the difficulty of this syllable-juncture sort, the teacher can gradually work other vowels into the sort until several short and long vowels are placed in the consonant-doubling or *e*-drop categories. Once these patterns are easily recognized, students can begin a two-column sort contrasting VCV (*bacon*) with VCCV (*common*) words.

Another useful type of reinforcement for these comparison/contrast activities is the **word hunt**. Whenever students are able to make correct decisions about the targeted word patterns during a sort, they can be asked to go to a given text and search for as many examples of the target patterns as they can find. These can be copied into a word-study notebook and labeled, and any exceptions to the basic pattern principle can be discussed and placed in a miscellaneous column. (Words that don't fit a predicted pattern shouldn't be labeled "exceptions." Many times such words fit within patterns that will be encountered later.)

As children move into the upper elementary grades, they confront a number of problems with vowels in unaccented syllables; for example, *-er, -ar,* and *-or* endings. In the unstressed condition, it is impossible to rely on sound clues to discern the correct vowel. To help students learn how to look at these words, the teacher can provide a **sample group** of words. The students arrange these words in columns by their pattern. A preliminary arrangement might look like this:

| doctor | lunar | fatter |
| spectator | regular | better |
| governor | angular | reader |
| mayor | spectacular | meaner |
| tractor | circular | cutter |
| | | runner |

With the words arranged in this fashion, the teacher then asks the students to look at the *-or* and *-ar* words and try to figure out what the words in each group have in common, that is, what meaning the ending gives the words. A likely explanation for *-or* is that it means someone or something that does something (whatever the stem indicates). Students may have more difficulty with *-ar*. If so, the teacher can show them that *-ar* means something like "having the characteristics of" whatever the word stem indicates. The last step would be to have the students divide the words in the *-er* column into two groups. They will most likely group the words as follows:

| fatter | reader |
| better | cutter |
| meaner | runner |

Students are then asked what they think are the two different meanings of *-er*. The comparative *-er* can be discussed—this spelling has no variations. The remaining words appear to function like *-or* to indicate someone or something that does what the base word indicates.

As students do more writing and proofreading, exercises of this kind can be very important in promoting spelling development. Word sorts help students develop an eye for pattern and sound relationships in our writing system. By highlighting various kinds of order in words, these activities can give students access to the elements of word knowledge necessary to bolster or advance their current stages of development.

# How To Assign Grades On A Daily Basis

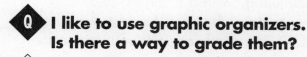

by Dr. Judy Wallis

K–12 Coordinator for Spring Branch Independent School District, Houston, Texas

As instructional practices change and new ways of assessing and evaluating students' progress are incorporated, most teachers are still faced with the task of giving grades. Although many teachers would prefer not to give grades, school districts and parents often insist on numerical or letter grades. The challenge is to find thoughtful ways to match these new practices with more traditional requirements. Here are some often-heard questions about grading:

**Q Aren't holistic scoring methods more subjective than traditional grades?**

**A** Actually, holistic scores can be very objective. By identifying the criteria *before* you score students' work, the grading is not subjective at all. For example, evaluation of journals can be done in the following way:

Criteria: Logs must

- be reflective.
- show learning.
- include a certain number of entries per week.

| Grading: | | |
|---|---|---|
| Consistently: | A or | 95% |
| Mostly: | B or | 85% |
| Sometimes: | C or | 75% |
| Rarely: | D or | 65% |

**Q I like to use graphic organizers. Is there a way to grade them?**

**A** Giving students guidelines before they complete the graphic organizer establishes the requirements and ensures fairness in grading. One teacher has students complete a character map after reading. Notice that the directions also include the score requirements:

*List five traits of the main character, and support each with examples from the story.*

| Grading | |
|---|---|
| 5 traits | = 90–100% |
| 4 traits | = 80–89% |
| 3 traits | = 70–79% |
| 2 traits | = 60–69% |
| 1 trait | = Below 60% |

**Q How do I grade my students' comprehension?**

**A** Retellings, summaries, and conferences can all be used to assess comprehension. Again, setting up the criteria with values before the students begin the activity is the key. You may want to consider using some of the following criteria: includes details, identifies the main idea or theme, refers to the text for support, makes inferences, and draws conclusions.

**Q** I think it is important for my students to grade themselves. Any suggestions?

**A** Self-evaluation is very important. People are required to assess themselves every day in the real world. Opportunities in school can occur in a variety of ways. Students can brainstorm the rubrics, or the teacher can decide on the criteria.

For example, students might decide that the rubrics for their literature responses should include creativity, evidence of careful planning, interest to others, and understanding of the story. Students would give 0–2 points per category and write a short justification for their score. The teacher or a classmate might also evaluate the response to provide perspective for the student. (Also, see page 123 for a form you can use or adapt to combine student and teacher evaluation on a regular basis.)

**Q** We spend a lot of time reading in my classroom. Is there a way to give my students credit for "just" reading?

**A** Yes! Simply establish reading goals for each grading period. If a student's goal is 5 books or 150 pages for a particular grading period, then 5 books or 150 pages would equal an A, 3–4 would equal a B, and so on. Certainly the goals might also include keeping a log, a certain number of response projects, and conferences with the teacher.

**Q** This all seems very time consuming. Doesn't it take longer than traditional grading?

**A** Because the activities are authentic and student-centered, they require less time to prepare. Students assume more responsibility and are doing more of the work. You will have time to offer thoughtful comments as you review students' work.

**Q** How can I help parents understand this new kind of grading?

**A** Most parents welcome the more authentic forms of assessment *once* they understand them. Communicating with parents *before* they have questions is imperative. Explain how you establish the criteria used to give grades, and they will be less likely to ask questions.

**Q** How can I get started?

**A** Read professionally. Start a study group with other teachers. Keep your eyes out for simple charts and checklists that you can modify for your needs.

It is always difficult to give up what feels safe and risk trying something new. However, the rewards are great. You will surely enjoy watching students become interested in more authentic tasks, develop the ability to evaluate themselves and to make thoughtful comments about the work of their peers, and grow as learners.

**Monday**  **Tuesday**  **Wednesday**  **Thursday**  **Friday**

**Student:** _____     **Date:** _____

## STUDENT'S DAILY REPORT

This is what I did to improve my reading: _____

_____

_____

_____

This is what I did to improve my writing: _____

_____

_____

_____

This is one new thing I learned today: _____

_____

_____

_____

This is one thing I did well with at least one other person: _____

_____

_____

_____

Other comments on today's learning: _____

_____

_____

_____

I think my grade for the day should be _____, because _____

_____

## TEACHER'S COMMENTS

_____

_____

_____

_____

Despite changes in instructional practices and new ways of assessing and evaluating children's progress, most teachers are still faced with the task of giving grades. Using a rubric such as the one shown below for rating a child's comprehension of a story, you can get a letter or numerical score on a holistic task. As long as you identify the criteria *before* you score children's work, the grading is not subjective at all.

---

### Story Comprehension

**Child** _____     **Date** _____

| | | | | |
|---|---|---|---|---|
| Child understands the story. | 4 | 3 | 2 | 1 |
| Child understands how main character feels. | 4 | 3 | 2 | 1 |
| Child recalls significant details. | 4 | 3 | 2 | 1 |
| Child notes cause-and-effect relationships. | 4 | 3 | 2 | 1 |
| Child generates questions and makes thoughtful comments. | 4 | 3 | 2 | 1 |

Totals      ___ + ___ + ___ + ___ = ___

_____ (score)

___ x 5 = ___

Score x 5 = comprehension total

**Comments** _____

_____

_____

_____

# A Look at Assessment

By Dr. Roger C. Farr
Chancellors' Professor of Education and Director of the Center for
Reading and Language Studies, Indiana University.

*"Alternative assessments seek to evaluate the processes of reading and writing."*

## Alternative Assessment

Alternative approaches to reading and writing assessment are being used in many schools across the United States. More than a response to criticism and concerns about the way that language development has usually been measured and the way that assessment results are used, these approaches attempt to match assessment to current language arts instruction, which emphasizes:

- an increasing reliance on children's literature as the primary text source.
- an integration of all language modes—particularly reading and writing—in language development activities.
- an understanding of language as a dynamic thinking process that draws on individual experiences, needs, and interests.
- a common-sense approach to developing language through student interaction and collaborative learning.
- a renewed trust in the judgments and ongoing evaluations of teachers, who can observe student progress daily and over long periods of time.
- the training of students to analyze their own thinking habits and skills as they read, write, and review collections of their written expression.

Traditional language tests have consisted of multiple-choice items that are classified by skill and subskill. Typically, the new types of reading assessment emerging today integrate reading and writing by having students compose a response to a text, which is often taken from children's literature. In facilitating these responses, the tests may offer optional activities that involve listening and speaking as well. Furthermore, like today's language instruction, current methods of assessment are founded on the idea that language should involve collaboration between students and interaction between students and texts. After all, language exists for the purpose of communication!

The emerging consensus is that assessment should reflect the interactive nature of reading. We can get a much better indication of how students comprehend if we observe how they respond to and discuss what they read. New approaches to observing student responses frequently promote individual student responses while encouraging student interaction and cooperation—even during assessment. Cooperation is an essential part of learning; it should be an essential part of assessment as well.

The new emphasis on interactive language and thinking processes has restored trust in teacher judgment. Assessments that mirror instruction can, like instruction, provide some structure and guidance; but the complex nature of the process is best evaluated by the teacher, who can observe a student's use of language daily.

The student, of course, has an even better opportunity to evaluate his or her own progress. Thus, the trends influencing language education today include an effort to make children aware of their own language use. This *metacognition* indelibly underlines the role of thinking in reading, listening, speaking, and writing. New evaluation techniques often draw on self-analysis of a student's responses to reading and of other expressions collected over time.

Over the past several years, teachers and schools have recognized the importance of process-oriented instruction. This concern with instructional process has emphasized the need for assessments that help teachers, and students themselves, understand the students' use of strategies to become effective readers and writers. This concern has led to the search for *alternative assessments;* that is, for alternatives to the multiple-choice tests that emphasize only correct answers or products. Alternative assessments seek to evaluate the *processes* of reading and writing. Alternative assessments can be either formal or informal.

> *"... **Put the emphasis in assessment squarely where it belongs: on what children know and** can do."*
>
> Dr. Roger Farr

## Why Informal Assessment Works

In discussing informal assessment, it is helpful to stress that the word *informal* means just what it usually does: casual, ordinary, and unceremonious. Informal assessment is *not* inferior to or less important than formal assessment in any way! It is, if anything, more important, for a host of good reasons:

- Informal assessment measures performance and achievement in its natural context—daily language use.

- It can, and should, occur every day—continuously and reiteratively. Thus, it serves both the teacher and the student on an ongoing basis to guide instruction and to establish evolving goals that result in helping the student become a better reader, writer, and thinker.

- It can be customized to match, reveal, and promote each student's particular growth patterns, strengths, needs, and interests.

- *Informal assessment should be an integral part of instruction!* Thus, special class time need not be set aside for it; assessment can be used as it is needed during the learning cycle as an integrated aspect of instruction.

- Good informal assessment provides diagnostic opportunities to identify strategies to be practiced, retaught, and extended on the basis of a particular student's abilities.

- Most importantly, perhaps, many types of informal assessment give the teacher the chance to involve the student as a *self-assessor,* an ultimate and enduring rationale for evaluating one's ability as a language user. In addition, students can use informal checklists to evaluate their peers' work and the work they do in *small groups.*

## Types of Informal Assessment

While the term *informal* appropriately refers to a broad range of assessments that teachers can use effectively and regularly, it is important, nonetheless, that teachers be somewhat systematic in using such assessments. Here are three general suggestions:

- Teachers should develop some sort of note-taking, or *recording,* technique that suits their own priorities and teaching strategies. This may be as simple as keeping one page or folder dedicated to each student or using self-stick notes to annotate copies of student writing.

- Whatever technique a teacher devises to record informal assessment, adding more information should be easy.

- The teacher should review the informal assessment information regularly and draw some summaries or conclusions that can direct future instruction.

In gathering information to analyze, there are several general principles that should guide the teacher as assessor:

- Informal assessment should always *encourage,* not discourage, all types of language use.

- The assessment should promote the student's sense of himself or herself as a writer, reader, speaker, and thinker. The object should never be to determine some grade or evaluation report for audiences other than the teacher or student.

- Such assessment should always be authentic; it should deal with *ideas* and *communications* of genuine concern and interest to the student. In general, informal assessment should *not* focus on mechanics.

- Informal assessment should provide information to be analyzed over a period of time and not be based on just one piece of writing or a single observation. It should be targeted to identifying patterns of student growth, development, and strength.

**CHILD'S NAME** _____

**TEACHER'S NAME**

_____

**GRADE** _____ **SCHOOL** _____

| MARKING KEY |
| --- |
| **+** Consistently |
| O Occasionally |
| — Never |

| | DATE | | | | | |
| --- | --- | --- | --- | --- | --- | --- |
| Tracks print successfully | | | | | | |
| Uses punctuation marks effectively | | | | | | |
| Applies basic phonetic generalizations and exceptions | | | | | | |
| Skips difficult words or phrases to stay focused on meaning | | | | | | |
| Rereads if things don't make sense | | | | | | |
| Self-corrects errors | | | | | | |
| Adds to the text only words that make sense contextually | | | | | | |
| Demonstrates a sense of story | | | | | | |

# Writitng Observational Checklist

**CHILD'S NAME** ______________________________

**TEACHER'S NAME** ______________________________

| MARKING KEY |
|---|
| + Consistently |
| O Occasionally |
| — Never |

| | DATE | | | | | |
|---|---|---|---|---|---|---|
| | | | | | | |
| Uses print as well as pictures to convey meaning | | | | | | |
| Writes from left to right | | | | | | |
| Leaves a space between words or groups of letters meant to represent words | | | | | | |
| Sounds out letters while writing words (i.e., shows an awareness that letters represent sounds and that words can be segmented into phonemes) | | | | | | |
| Displays an awareness of grammar when writing sentences | | | | | | |
| Displays an awareness of punctuation | | | | | | |
| Evaluates his or her writing or drawing and the writing or drawing of peers | | | | | | |

**COMMENTS** ______________________________

______________________________

______________________________

CHILD'S NAME _____

TEACHER'S NAME _____

| MARKING KEY |
| --- |
| **+** Consistently |
| **O** Occasionally |
| **—** Never |

**DATE**

| | | | | | |
| --- | --- | --- | --- | --- | --- |
| | | | | | |

**Speaking**

| | | | | | |
| --- | --- | --- | --- | --- | --- |
| Volunteers for speaking activities | | | | | |
| Makes comments that are appropriate to the situation | | | | | |
| Expresses ideas clearly and accurately | | | | | |
| Uses information accurately | | | | | |
| Supports point of view with logical evidence | | | | | |
| Responds logically to comments of others | | | | | |
| Rephrases or adjusts if others don't understand | | | | | |
| Takes turns in group discussions | | | | | |

**Listening**

| | | | | | |
| --- | --- | --- | --- | --- | --- |
| Attends to what others are saying | | | | | |
| Exhibits reactions (e.g., facial expressions) that reflect comprehension | | | | | |
| Understands directions without needing repetition | | | | | |
| Ignores distractions | | | | | |

© Harcourt

COMMENTS _____

STUDENT _____

TIME PERIOD: from _____ to _____

How does the student evaluate his or her own reading?

How much reading has he or she done during this period?

How does this amount of reading compare with that done in the previous period?

Which pieces of reading seem to have interested the student the most?

Are there signs of new or developing interests?

What goals can I recommend to this student for the next period?

Are there any particular books, stories, or informational texts I can recommend?

What should we discuss in the next student-teacher conference?

© Harcourt

STUDENT _____

TIME PERIOD: from _____ to _____

How does the student evaluate his or her own writing?

How much writing has he or she done during this period?

How does this amount of writing compare with that done in the previous period?

What types, or genres, of writing did the student write during this period? Is there evidence of change in topics or genres preferred? What are some examples?

Is there a growing sense of story structure—beginning, middle, ending?

Is sentence or clause structure and use of connectors more sophisticated than before?

What evidence is there of a developing style and voice?

Is the student aware of audiences? Which ones?

Has control of mechanics and usage improved? If so, how?

What goals can I recommend for this student for the next period?

© Harcourt

# Running Records, Kid Watching, Anecdotal Records, & Benchmarks

## by DR. ROGER C. FARR

**The most useful information you can collect about your students' reading is the information you gather as part of regular instruction and during the reading of literature selections. This kind of assessment provides information about how students actually read text and what they do during class time. Running records, kid watching, and the collecting of anecdotal records are three common methods for engaging in this kind of informal assessment.**

## Running Records

A running record is a procedure you can use to learn about a student's oral reading.[1] The goal is to learn as much as you can about the student's reading strategies. You simply have a student read aloud, and while the student is reading, you record everything that the student says and does.

[1] The concept of a running record was developed by Marie Clay and is explained more fully in her book *An Observation: Survey of Early Literacy Achievement,* Portsmouth, NH: Heinemann, 1993.

The best approach is to have a student choose a story or another type of selection that he or she would *like* to read. You will need either a copy of the story the child reads so that you can record the student's reading, or a form like the one on page 136, which will help you record the reading, or both. Running records are usually based on a student's reading of 100 to 200 words. If you have a copy of the selection, mark the selection as directed on page 134. When the student is finished reading, you should check his or her comprehension by discussing the selection or by asking the student to tell you about the selection.

After the running-record activity is completed, you will be able to review it and note the student's reading strategies and miscue patterns. See page 134 for an explanation of miscues.

By paying attention to both the miscues and the student's comprehension of the text, you can determine a great deal about a student's use of reading strategies to construct meaning. This information can be very valuable in planning reading instruction. In addition, by collecting these running records over the course of a semester, you can determine how effective your instruction has been and how the student is developing as a strategic reader.

| Marking Oral Reading Miscues | | |
|---|---|---|
| **Reading Miscue** | **Marking** | **Sample** |
| 1. omissions | Circle the word, word part, or phrase omitted. | I will let you (go) in. |
| 2. insertions | Insert a caret ( ∧ ), and write in the inserted word or phrase. | We bought a ∧big parrot. |
| 3. substitutions | Write the word or phrase the student substitutes over the word or phrase in the text. | Dad fixed ~~my~~ the bike. |
| 4. mispronunciations | Write the phonetic mispronunciation over the word. | Have you ~~fed~~ feed the dog? |
| 5. self-corrections | Write the letters *SC* next to the miscue that is self-corrected. | We took our ~~spote~~ space. SC |
| 6. repetitions | Draw a line under any part of the text that is repeated. | It is your <u>garden</u> now. |
| 7. punctuation | Circle punctuation missed. Write in any punctuation inserted. | Take them home(.)Then come back, and you and I will go to town. |
| 8. hesitations | Place vertical lines at places where the student hesitates excessively. | Pretend \|this is mine. |

# Kid Watching

A term that has gained great popularity in integrated language arts assessment is *kid watching*. The phrase is attributed to Yetta Goodman, who believes that if teachers are to understand children's language development, they must become thoughtful observers of how children use language.

Kid watching means that teachers observe children as they engage in all kinds of language activities, both during instruction and as they read and write. However, just watching is not useful unless the teacher knows what to look for and how to observe.

Kid watching as assessment must focus on how children use language and how they develop as readers and writers. The watching must not be a watching that interferes and asks questions. Rather, it must be a watching that allows children to engage in realistic language activities and notes what kinds of problems they encounter and how they deal with those problems. For example, noting what a child does when he or she comes to an unfamiliar word or observing how a child works out a story event that he or she doesn't seem to understand can provide the kind of information that a dedicated kid-watcher looks for.

# Anecdotal Records

Anecdotal records are nothing more than the notes you make about the things that you see when you are working with your students. You notice all kinds of things, and these can be recorded and saved so that you can go back through them at a later time to discern patterns of development, specific needs that will help you plan instruction, or evidence that new concepts are being applied.

Your anecdotal records will be more effective if you collect them systematically. You may want to focus on specific skills or strategies for a week and observe how those are being used. Don't try to observe everything. Focused observation on a few essential skills or strategies will be much more effective than collecting lots of information about everything. Not only will such note-taking interfere with your teaching but also you will probably not have time to read through the notes and determine what they are telling you.

There are many ways to collect anecdotal records. Here are just a few ideas used by some effective teachers:

- A spiral-bound notebook with several pages set aside for each child in your class can provide an easy system for collecting anecdotal records about students' writing. These notes can include observations about the kinds of questions children ask as they go about their writing, their effectiveness working in groups, and their use of classroom resources to gather writing ideas.

- Self-stick notes are an easy way to collect annotations about children's language skills. They can be written rapidly (use initials or first names to speed up the process) and stuck to *Teacher's Edition* pages on which you are working or on the page in your lesson plan book that relates to that activity.

- Self-stick notes can also be attached directly to student papers. You can write them as students are working on a writing project. Then later, when the papers are collected for your review, you can add the self-stick notes to the appropriate papers.

- Some teachers dictate notes into a tape recorder for later transcription (or simply for use as an oral record). You can dictate quickly at the end of a class period or at a break time. Later, you can take notes by listening to your recording.

There are many other possibilities for collecting information as you work with your students. The best ones are usually developed by you, the teacher, to fit your style, your classroom organization, and your students' needs.

# Benchmarks

Benchmarks are like road signs that tell you where you are. These benchmarks are general indicators as to what a student should be learning and be able to do if he or she is to be a successful reader and writer. By focusing on specific benchmarks, you can better help each student achieve success with them throughout the year.

These benchmarks provide guidance for the things you should be observing. There are numerous ways to informally assess your students' progress in achieving these benchmarks. When you review their reading and writing activities and when you engage in kid watching you will find specific examples of the benchmarks. It is not important to assess the benchmarks as isolated behaviors. Each of the benchmarks is related to other language behaviors and should be observed as they are exhibited by your students as they read and write.

## Miscue Analysis Summary Form

Name _____  Grade _____  Date _____

Teacher _____  Level Administered _____

**1.** *Number of Miscues*          Error rate: _____

   Comments: _____

   _____

   _____

**2.** *Type of Miscues*          No. of meaning-based miscues _____

                          No. of graphic/sound-based miscues _____

   Comments and patterns observed: _____

   _____

**3.** *Self-Corrections*          No. of self-corrections _____

   Comments: _____

   _____

   _____

**4.** *Fluency*     Check one: _____ High _____ Moderate _____ Low

   Comments: _____

   _____

   _____

Summary of strengths: _____

_____

_____

Summary of weaknesses: _____

_____

_____

# Think-Alongs: Comprehension Strategies Assessment By Dr. Roger C. Farr

Think-along assessment is an informal assessment technique, similar to running records and reading miscue analyses, that focuses on how students think while reading and whether they are learning to construct meaning. Instead of merely asking students to read aloud, you also ask them to tell what they are thinking about while reading. Their reading comprehension improves because the strategy actually encourages them to construct meaning. Many teachers use think-along not just as an assessment strategy but also as an instructional activity.

To use the strategy with an individual student, follow these steps:

- Select an interesting story or article that will enable the student to use background knowledge along with other reading strategies.
- Mark the text with a red dot at points where the reader might make a prediction, decide how an event or character looks, or use some background knowledge to explain what is happening. As students gain experience, they will say what they are thinking at points that seem reasonable to them, and the red dots will no longer be necessary.
- Have the students read aloud, stopping at each red dot to tell what he or she is thinking. Model the technique for students who are unfamiliar with it.
- Record on copies of the blackline master provided on page 139 the phrases the student uses to think aloud. You may want to write the phrases on a sheet of paper and later transfer them to the form. (A partially completed form for a student's reading and telling of *Rummage Sale,* by Barbara Jossee, is included.)

- When the student has finished reading, follow up with a discussion of any issues that may have been confusing or that you would like to have the student expand on.
- After the session, use your notes and strategy categories to determine how well the student read, what strategies were used, and whether the strategies were used effectively. You can also assess the student's reading on a scale of 1 to 5, with 5 indicating good understanding and effective use of a wide range of comprehension strategies.

A comprehension strategy analysis takes no more time than a reading miscue analysis or a running record. Categorizing the think-aloud phrases as specific strategies may seem confusing at first. However, more important than the categorization of the strategies is an attempt to see whether a student uses a variety of strategies and is able to construct meaning while reading.

This informal assessment strategy can also be used with an entire class. First, reformat a selection so that it flows down one side of a page in a single column. On the other side of the page, students write what they are thinking as they read. Use red dots in the text to mark points at which students are to stop and write. As with the oral think-along, encourage them to write when they have something they want to say.

Though written think-alongs may not provide as rich a base for analysis as individual oral assessments, the written technique allows you to assess many more students at one time and has been used successfully by many teachers.

Here is a partial analysis for a student whose name is Hana. The blackline master on page 139 can be copied and modified for use in your classroom.

## THINK-ALONG STRATEGIES

**Directions:**
As you observe the think-along process, identify the phrases used by the student that indicate a reading strategy. Match these phrases with the strategies listed below. Use as few words as possible to indicate the teaching strategies.

| Strategies | Identifying Phrases |
|---|---|
| **Purpose** | Selection: Rummage Sale, by Barbara Jossee <br> Find out about a yard sale. |
| **Prediction** | Nobody is going to buy that baby. <br> I don't think the girl will change the boy's mind. <br> I am sure she will change her mind about selling the baby. |
| **Identify with Characters** | I think she is just jealous. <br> I am surprised her mother isn't mad at her (for trying to sell the baby). |

I would rate Hana 5 on a scale of 1 to 5. She uses a wide variety of strategies, and she definitely knows what is going on. The questions she raises about the rattle and the lady saying "widdle beebee" are probably about differences in culture.

It would have been good if Hana had read some of the story to see whether she could find the answer to her own question about where the girl got the money for the bean bag game.

The two strategies that Hana used the most were personal experience and recognizing confusion. She related a lot from the story to experiences she has had.

© Harcourt

# THINK-ALONG STRATEGIES

**Directions:**
As you observe the think-along process, identify the phrases used by the student that indicate a reading strategy. Match these phrases with the strategies listed below. Use as few words as possible to indicate the teaching strategies.

| Strategies | Identifying Phrases |
|---|---|
| **Purpose** | |
| **Prediction** | |
| **Identify with Characters** | |
| **Personal Experience** | |
| **Visualize** | |
| **Review Ideas** | |
| **Reread** | |
| **Restate** | |
| **Summarize** | |
| **Elaborate** | |
| **Recognize Confusion** | |
| **Skip Around** | |
| **Context Clues** | |
| **Concentrate** | |

# Assessing Emergent Writers

by Dr. Roger C. Farr

**A**ssessment of emergent writing is, quite simply, the thoughtful and appreciative observation of how children express themselves with pictures and symbols. Because what the child wants to say is not always immediately apparent from the marks he or she has put on the paper, this assessment also requires the evaluator to *listen* to the child's ideas about his or her writing. These conversations should encourage the child to become a self-assessor.

*"Assessment is directly linked to instruction and is in itself instructional."*

**Q.** **What are the typical forms of emergent writing?**

**A.** *Picture drawing as a kind of language*
Anyone who has talked with very young children about their drawings knows that these pictures have meaning just as surely as a written or oral story that is represented by the pictures. The pictures often present ideas and rich details that go beyond the verbal story.

*Scribble writing* As children experience more and more literacy events, they begin to understand that the black marks on a page next to a picture carry meaning. And so they begin to mimic those symbols by pretend or scribble writing. To the child, however, this scribbling is just as surely writing as is the print on a page. Often these "scribbles" include both odd-shaped letters and pictures woven together. The scribble writing may extend horizontally, from left to right, and with some erratic sense of margins and placement on a page.

*Letter strings* At some point, young writers begin stringing together letters and shapes that approximate letters, frequently within a line of scribbling. These letters have been observed by the child in signs and books and on TV; often, too, children have had exposure to them in school activities. Some children will tie drawings into this very early writing in fascinating attempts to communicate.

*Invented spelling* Children surrounded by print and familiar with the alphabet will eventually begin to tie letter sounds to individual letters in order to communicate more effectively. Given ample opportunity to read and write, alone and within a group, children feel free to take risks in how they spell words.

**Q.** **How can I read scribble writing?**

**A.** *Have the child read it to you! Observational research has demonstrated that many children can retell their stories—following their scribbling—in much the same way they tell them as they scribble. This suggests that for them the scribbling has more literal representation than may be presumed. Don't be concerned that the story is longer or shorter than the scribble writing seems to indicate. Also, don't be concerned that the story changes each time the child tells it. The important point is that you and the child get a sense that the marks on the page can and do represent a story.*

**Q.** **When does conventional spelling begin?**

**A.** *It actually begins with the use of letter strings. These are conventional spellings, often in fairly consistent patterns. However, they are not the spelling forms that are acceptable to the public. Those acceptable spellings will come naturally as children read and write more. For the vast majority of children, you'll see a definite progression toward more and more conventional spelling, idea structures, and punctuation particularly when children enjoy daily, intense exposure to print. The content, too, becomes more semantically and syntactically acceptable. The teacher can watch for other signs of progress as well. For example, the child begins to use words that relate ideas temporally, spatially, and in other ways. The complexity of the stories told and ideas expressed, the emergence of a distinctive writer's "voice," and attempts at conventions such as dialogue develop along with more mechanical concerns such as spelling and capitalization.*

**Q.** Some of my children seem to use several forms of writing within the same piece. Should I be concerned about this?

**A.** *Researchers have documented developmental sequences in which drawing and different types of writing/printing may appear. However, these sequences can vary according to the individual child and that child's experience with language. Conventional writing doesn't develop in a rigid hierarchical sequence; children may move back and forth among several writing forms as they experiment with what they already know and what they have just learned. Also, the amount of time that a child wants to devote to a particular piece will influence the forms he or she uses.*

**Q.** What about assessing content, specifically, a child's ability to string together story events and his or her choice of words?

**A.** *Evaluators certainly want to know about an emergent writer's sense of story: elements such as logical ordering of events, character development, and cause and effect. Children will vary tremendously in their ability to include a beginning, a middle, and an ending; again, these concepts don't develop in a predictable, linear fashion. It is best to listen to what the child says about his or her story; the complexity of his or her ideas will probably surprise you!*

*Whether a child has a sense of story can be determined with oral retellings of favorite stories that have been read to or with the child. Listen for similarities to the stories you have been reading to the children. Some children will be more proficient users of story elements and will use a much richer vocabulary to retell story events. However, as you read and discuss more and more stories, you will find that all of your children are developing a greater knowledge of story elements.*

*Being the singular individual that they are, children devise unique ways to convey information that is important to them. Given the freedom and encouragement to do so, the child will develop a kind of individualistic writing style as his or her own voice.*

**Q.** Some of my children seem unsure of their own writing and insist on dictating their stories to me. How can I assess these?

**A.** *You have a wonderful opportunity to find out about the child's reading and to emphasize with the child that writing is talk written down. Write the story for the child and then have him or her read it back to you. You will learn a great deal about story knowledge and reading development this way. (By the way, help the child with any words he or she does not know.) If you continue this type of activity, it won't be long before the reluctant writer is beginning to pen his or her own stories. This is an excellent example of how good assessment and good instruction tie together naturally.*

**Q.** I really hesitate to judge young children's efforts, especially children who are just beginning to take risks in their writing. Should I be correcting all of the "errors" I see in their writing? Should I attempt to put a grade on their papers?

**A.** *The answer to both questions is an unequivocal NO! You're absolutely right to be concerned about the message you're sending emerging writers when you "grade" their work. Instead, think of your role as being an encouraging guide. Basically, your task is to be watching (really, with young children, you're doing more listening) for the student's developing awareness of himself or herself as a writer communicating with particular audiences! For this to occur, the child must be given ample opportunity to talk about the things he or she is writing and the teacher must observe over a period of time. A teacher who regards assessment as a kind of encouraging, benign guidance is doing the very best for children.*

*We have learned from research and classroom practice that when emerging writers are concerned about making mistakes, their growth in writing stops! Suddenly, they're constantly asking how to spell a word, whether this is the right way to say something, and where to put capital letters and periods. Concern with telling a story and taking risks with language is lost, and growth in writing is surely stunted.*

## Q. How is all of this assessment used?

**A.** *Perhaps the most dangerous concept about assessment is that it is done separately from instruction. Good assessment is part of instruction. The observations you make, the notes you take, and the discussions you have with students are the "stuff" of assessment. What you learn about your group of emerging writers should immediately impact the kinds of literacy experiences you provide in your classroom. For example, suppose you feel that several children show a weak sense of story. You would then make a special effort to include discussions of the beginning, middle, and ending of stories they are reading. Or, if your children exhibit a limited awareness of the audience for whom they write, you might expand their opportunities for sharing with other age groups. This is the best way for them to experience first-hand the importance of keeping the audience in mind during the writing process.*

All children have an important story to tell and a voice as individualistic as any adult's. This deserves our utmost respect. By focusing primarily on children's ideas, but also watching for and guiding the increasing use of language conventions, we put the emphasis in assessment squarely where it belongs: on what children know and *can* do. More importantly, our efforts should always emphasize helping children understand their writing development. As they begin to self-assess their writing, they are developing into writers who always consider the needs and purposes of their audiences.

### Basic Guidelines to Remember

1. Assessment is directly linked to instruction and is in itself instructional.
2. Always assess what the child *can* do. Give every child a chance to be successful.
3. Listen to the language children use to talk about their writing. This by itself reveals a great deal about their development as writers.
4. Help children become self-assessors. Look for a growing understanding of the functions of reading and writing.
5. Try not to think of reading and writing as separate assessments. A child's literacy development includes both reading and writing, as well as oral language. Don't compartmentalize your assessment. Make sure the assessment of writing helps you and the child to make connections between all of the language arts.
6. Look for growth *over time* in a writer's awareness of
   - audience and purpose.
   - story elements—character; setting; story problem; beginning, middle, ending; dialogue; etc.
   - print conventions—word spacing, letterforms, punctuation, capital letters, etc.
7. Encourage children to take risks. This is how they come to use more conventional forms of writing.

# Assessing the Phonics Skills of Beginning Readers with a Performance Assessment

by Dr. Roger C. Farr

**A**performance assessment given at kindergarten or at the beginning of first grade that asks a student to write will provide information about a student's understanding of the story. It can also be an excellent means to determine how well the student is developing his or her ability to use phonic skills.

### Using the Book *"That Bothered Kate"*

One of the performance assessments developed for beginning readers is based on *That Bothered Kate,* a delightful story by Sally Noll. After they listen to the story, students are asked to draw and write about what bothered Kate. The story is about two sisters, Kate and Tory. Tory is the younger sister and like many younger sisters, she adores her older sister and copies everything she does. Later in the story Tory develops other friendships and she doesn't copy Kate as often—and that bothers Kate. The story has a happy ending as Mom explains that this is all part of growing up.

Students who have completed the task have drawn a variety of pictures that tell what bothered Kate. Through their drawings they have demonstrated their understanding of the story as well as their ability to convey their understanding to another person.

## Using the Assessment for Phonics Diagnosis

A student's writing can be an excellent source of information about his or her developing knowledge of the relationship between spoken and written language. This is true even if the student does not write anything at all. Here are the steps you need to follow to conduct this diagnosis:

- Soon after the students have completed their drawings and any writing they may have added to the picture, ask them to read aloud what they have written. If they seem bothered by being asked to read what they have written, then ask them to tell about their pictures.

- This should be done as soon as possible after the assessment (at least on the same day) and should be done on a one-to-one basis. If students overhear what others have to say, they will tend to repeat without attention to what they have written.

- Do not write on the student's paper what the student says as this may leave the child with the impression that he or she cannot write and that you have to write for them.

- As soon as you can find a moment, write down on a note pad exactly what the student has said. The relationship between what the student wrote, including the picture, and what he or she says is the information you will use for diagnosis.

- Be sure you are focused on what you want to find out. The assessment will tell you how well the student understood the story, but your phonic assessment is focused on learning about the student's beginning phonic skills.

## Phonic Skills That Can Be Assessed

The beginning phonic skills, that are important to beginning reading and that can be determined from this assessment, include the following:

1. Does the student understand that letters make meaning? That is, does the student attempt to write and then to read the words he or she has written?

2. Does the student understand the difference between letters and words? In his or her writing, does the student include spaces between words? Does the student point to the words he or she has written as he or she reads them?

3. Did the student attempt to write (encode) what he or she wanted to say?

4. Did the student attempt to read (decode) what he or she had written?

5. Did the student's writing and reading what he or she had written indicate knowledge of the relationship between beginning phonemes (sounds) and graphemes (letters)?

6. Did the student's writing and reading what he or she had written indicate knowledge of the relationship between ending phonemes (sounds) and graphemes (letters)?

7. Did the student's writing and reading what he or she had written indicate knowledge of the relationship between medial phonemes (sounds) and graphemes (letters)?

## Applying the Diagnosis

On the page that follows there are four student papers. Beside each is exactly what the student said when he or she read. Each student's ability to use each of the seven phonic skills identified above is summarized in a table following the student responses.

The scoring for the diagnosis is on a three-point scale. A (3) indicates the student is quite accomplished at the skill, a (2) indicates the student seems to have some knowledge of the skill, and a (1) indicates that the student is not using the skill at all or only to a very limited extent.

| | |
|---|---|
|  | Eduardo read, *"Her sister is copying riding the scooter."*<br><br>Eduardo did not point to the letters at the top of his drawing when he read. When asked about the letters, he said they were there because he wanted to write about the story. |
|  | Maryann read, *"Katy's sister copied her dressing up."*<br><br>Maryann pointed to the first word and said, "That's my name, Maryann." When Maryann read "dressing up," she pointed to the crossed out ending to *DRSE* and said she didn't know how to write that word and then pointed to *DRSIP* and said, "that's dressing up." |
|  | Leticia read, *"What bothered Kate was they wore the same clothes."*<br><br>What is interesting about this writing/reading is the relationship between what was written and the picture. It seems clear from what Leticia read and from what she wrote, that after she read "What bothered Kate," her picture supplied the rest of the sentence, "was they wore the same clothes." |
|  | Henry read, *"What bothered Kate—Tory!"*<br><br>It was very interesting to note how Henry emphasized the word *Tory* in both his reading and writing. |

## Scoring the Assessment

The diagnostic profile below indicates a rating for each of the four students on the eight beginning phonic skills that can be assessed with this process. While you may not be in total agreement with each of the scores, you can see how the assessment gives you a good idea as to what the students know and don't know about the relationship between what they wrote and how they read their writing.

## Summary Table

|  | Eduardo | Maryann | Leticia | Henry |
|---|---|---|---|---|
| 1. Understands that letters make meaning. | 2 | 3 | 3 | 3 |
| 2. Distinguishes one word from another. | 1 | 3 | 1 | 2 |
| 3. Attempts to write (encodes). | 1 | 3 | 2 | 3 |
| 4. Attempts to read what was written (decodes). | 1 | 3 | 2 | 3 |
| 5. Matches initial letters with sounds. | 1 | 3 | 2 | 2 |
| 6. Matches final letters with sounds. | 1 | 3 | 2 | 1 |
| 7. Matches medial letters with sounds. | 1 | 1 | 1 | 1 |
| Total beginning phonics diagnosis. | 8 | 19 | 13 | 15 |

It is easy to tell from the summary table who has the most well-developed phonics skills and which students are not yet grasping the relationship between spoken words and written symbols. It is also easy to see that most of these students have a well-developed sense of the idea that written symbols can be used to tell a story. The area where they are most lacking is their ability to match medial sounds of words with corresponding letters and they do far better matching initial and final sounds with corresponding letters.

# Reading/ Writing PORTFOLIOS

## by DR. ROGER C. FARR

One important example of the focus on process assessment in the language arts is the widely spreading emphasis on *the use of portfolios as an alternative assessment.* In this approach, students collect, organize, and analyze numerous samples of their own work. Assessment becomes instruction because students learn to assess *themselves.* In many classrooms, they do so in response to their personal goals, objectives, needs, and interests.

Teaching methods that integrate reading and writing often have students develop working portfolios that include their responses to literature. Working portfolios include manuscripts showing various stages of the writing process. Portfolio collections reflect many classroom activities and reveal a student's new understanding, intriguing ideas, feelings, beliefs, and concerns.

Students select a variety of types of writing for their portfolios to demonstrate their progress as thinkers and language users and their individual approaches to and styles of writing. At the same time, the portfolios are a record of texts each student has read and an indication of the use the student has made of particular texts.

Working portfolios should also include reading logs and other responses to literature, including original efforts that reading has inspired, as well as samples from journals and notes taken in response to reading and in interviews with peers, parents, and others. Since much of the portfolio contains writing that can be done in response to reading, the student's writing begins to reveal the student's grasp of and attitude about the use of literature as a model for the student's own writing.

As students compile their selected writings, they are conducting an extensive self-assessment of their own progress. The prime analysts of the material are each student and the teacher, but portfolios can also be used effectively when discussing student progress with administrators and with parents or guardians.

Because portfolios focus on individual students and their responses to reading and other experiences, portfolios depend on relatively subjective analysis. There is nothing wrong with that! For some teachers, it might be the first real ongoing opportunity they have structured for this kind of assessment. The portfolio is so personal, in fact, that it ensures individualized instruction.

# Portfolio Conferences

## BY DR. ROGER C. FARR

### Portfolio Conference Guidelines

A conference is an essential step in the portfolio process. During a conference, you should attempt to do two things. First, you want to learn all you can about the student's reading and writing interests, habits, and abilities. Second, you want to help the student reflect on his or her own reading and writing activities and take responsibility for improvement. The outcome of a successful conference should include the formation of specific instructional goals. (You may want to use the forms on pages 131 and 132 to keep records of student-teacher conferences. These records could be kept in your own folder for each student.)

The goals that are established will be different for each student, because each conference will be different and personal. Students may want to expand reading interests in a variety of ways: for example, reading about certain topics or reading books by favorite authors. These goals will naturally grow out of conferences if you allow students the time to talk about the reading and writing they have been doing.

### Finding Time for Portfolio Conferences

Many types of portfolio conferences can be conducted with relatively little time spent. These include impromptu conferences, in which students discuss a writing project or a reading selection with the teacher; group conferences, in which students meet to share some information and goals; and peer conferences.

However, it is important to have periodic *planned and scheduled individual conferences with each student in your classroom.* Try to allow for a minimum of four of these each year. Each individual conference should take about fifteen minutes. Some will be longer, and some will be shorter. This means that you are going to spend a total of about one hour of scheduled individual conference time with each student over the course of the entire year. With all the other demands on your time and energy, this will not be easy. However, the benefits of individual conferences are worth the time and effort. Some suggestions to help you "find" the time for portfolio conferences follow.

| General Organization/Structure | Specific Suggestions |
|---|---|
| Have someone work with the other students while you conference with individual students. If you do have assistance available, you should **not** turn the portfolio conferencing over to the person who helps you. Conferences are so important to you as a teacher that your personal time with each student must be protected. | **Teacher aides** are available in some schools, and they provide a useful resource.<br><br>**Parents** and family members are sometimes willing to serve as teacher helpers, who may talk with the students about their interests, read to the students, or engage in some other appropriate activity while you are holding conferences.<br><br>**Team teaching** activities provide ideal opportunities. You and a fellow teacher can plan some large-group activities, during which the two of you can take turns working with the total group of students while one of you conducts individual student conferences. |
| Many of the literacy activities in an integrated reading/writing program provide conferencing time. 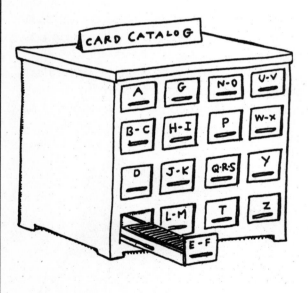 | While some students are engaged in **literature circles,** you can conduct several portfolio conferences with other students.<br><br>The time during which students are engaged in **writer's workshop** activities is another good portfolio conference time.<br><br>**Library visits** are usually a key part of an integrated program, and while students are engaged in library research, you can meet with individual students.<br><br>You may find time to conduct one or two conferences during **journal writing** time.<br><br>It is very useful to have students write their thoughts about their portfolios before they confer with you. During this **self-evaluation time,** you can conduct several conferences. |
| Outside-of-class time can be used if you can get the schedules, both yours and the students', to coincide. | Some school systems provide short periods either **before or after** school for teachers to meet with individual students.<br><br>If students have **study periods** or other flexible time in their schedules, you can plan to meet with them during those times. |

| General Organization/Structure | Specific Suggestions |
|---|---|

You can also work the portfolio conferences into your regular instructional time.

Giving students the responsibility to find the time to meet with you works well in some classes. In using these suggestions, you will not be solving the time problem, but you will be sharing the responsibility with your students.

Some teachers utilize **learning centers** as a regular part of instruction. One of these can be developed into a portfolio center, where individual students meet with you while other students are engaged at other learning centers.

**Peer tutoring** can be scheduled along with buddy reading or shared reading, conferencing about written pieces, or developing special projects. During these peer-tutoring times, portfolio conferences can be your peer-tutoring activity.

**Sustained silent reading** is a time when all students (and the teacher) are to be reading silently. You may want to occasionally use that time to schedule portfolio conferences.

Many teachers plan a variety of class activities in which students work independently or in small groups. These include such activities as doing research for a project, preparing art materials for a story or poem, and self-selection of a reading or writing activity. During these **independent class activities,** you can plan to conduct several portfolio conferences.

**Learning contracts** can be developed in which one aspect of the contract is that a student must schedule an appointment (for example, sometime in the next week) to discuss his or her reading/writing portfolio with you.

Post a **sign-up sheet,** and tell students that they must sign up for portfolio conference time during the scheduled times.

Develop a **portfolio-picnic** program. Have children sign up for lunch with you (or draw names out of a hat). After lunch (during which you could discuss favorite books), you could spend ten minutes discussing the portfolio. In two weeks, you could do ten conferences.

| General Organization/Structure | Specific Suggestions |
|---|---|
| If you have tried some of the ideas above and are still struggling to find time for portfolio conferences, here are some suggestions.<br><br> | Start out with **small-group conferences.** Use these groups to give each student an opportunity to discuss his or her portfolio. Small-group conferences tend to be less effective than individual conferences, but they are a way to get started.<br><br>**Peer conferences** are best held *after* you have conducted many individual student-teacher conferences. Peer conferences are of limited value if the students have not already experienced in-depth discussions with the teacher. Try modeling an effective conference with one or two students while the rest of the class listens and watches.<br><br>Have a **dialogue conference**. Ask each student to write notes about his or her port-folio, and then collect the portfolios and notes. After reviewing the contents of the portfolio, write a response to what each student has written.<br><br>Have students take their portfolios to a learning center (which could be a table at the back of the room) equipped with a **tape recorder.** Have each student review the contents of his or her portfolio and tell you (through a taped message) about each item in it. You can listen to the recording and leave a recorded response to the student's message.<br><br>Plan a **two-stage approach** to conferences. Have the students hold peer conferences before (or after) they confer with you. If the peer conferences are held before, they give the students an opportunity to get their ideas together before meeting with you. If they are held after your conference, they give the student an opportunity to get their ideas together before meeting with you. If they are held after your conference, they give the student an opportunity to expand on ideas you have started by talking with another student. During the peer conferences in this two-stage conference time, you can confer with individual students. |

## Portfolio Conference Guidelines

Portfolio conferences are really quite simple. All you have to do is remember that a conference is a time for sharing and that you are having a conversation with a person who has much to offer. The following guidelines outline some of the essentials:

- **Let the child do most of the talking.** You will learn much more about the child if you let him or her talk.

- **Avoid being evaluative.** Respect the child as a learner. If you think of the conference as a time for the child to reflect on his or her own reading and writing, you will be less judgmental.

- **Avoid interruptions.** Children need undivided attention during a conference. If you are constantly interrupted, the child will be unable to develop his or her ideas. Also, if you allow constant interruptions, the child may conclude that this one-to-one discussion is not very important to you.

- **Ask questions that open up conversations rather than shut down communication.** Use open-ended questions that ask for explana-tions, expansions, examples, and discussion. You learn more about children when they explain, justify, clarify, and express their ideas and beliefs. The quality of the responses will depend on the quality of the questions you ask. Children will provide more explanations if they believe that you are interested in and truly respect them and their opinions.

- **Use the conference as a time to plan goals with the child.** Ask questions such as the following: What do you plan to read or write about next? What are you planning to do with this story? How can I help you?

- **Write notes about what you have learned.** Take time after each conference to jot down notes about the conference and the goals you and the child have discussed. Add the notes to the child's portfolio so they can be reviewed at the next conference.

## CONFERENCE CHECKLIST

### Reading and Writing Focus

☐ gives the most important purpose for reading and writing

☐ is willing to share ideas

☐ shows confidence and takes risks in experimenting with new ideas

☐ uses information from other models, from other authors and genres, or from friends

☐ explores personal interests through reading and writing

☐ is aware of audience

### Reading and Writing Strategies and Conventions

☐ indicates sources of ideas, such as personal experiences or reading

☐ gives evidence of how feedback from others has been incorporated into reading and writing

☐ uses expressive language to discuss a previously read book or a selected piece of writing

☐ connects ideas logically in organizational schemes such as comparison and contrast, cause and effect, or time sequence

| GENERAL QUESTION/STATEMENT | FOLLOW-UP QUESTIONS |
| --- | --- |
| **1. Tell me how you use your portfolio.** | Why did you organize your portfolio this way?<br>How did you decide which pieces to include in your portfolio? |
| **2. Tell me about one story in your portfolio.** | Why is this story important to you?<br>Why did you choose to write this?<br>Where did you get the idea?<br>Would you like to read it to me?<br>Did you have any problem writing it? |
| **3. Tell me about a book that you have read.** | Explain to me why this book is important to you. Why did you decide to read this book?<br>Why would someone else like reading it? |
| **4. What are you going to read and write next?** | How can I help you with this?<br>What will you do first?<br>Is there someone with whom you would like to work? |

© Harcourt

**Child's Name** _____

**Teacher's Name** _____

**Grade** _____ **School** _____

**Date of Reading Conference** _____

Name someone who is a good reader. Why do you think so?

_____

What do you do before you begin to read?

_____

What do you do when you see a word you don't know?

_____

What do you do when something doesn't make sense to you when you are reading?

_____

What do you do when you need help while you are reading?

_____

What is the hardest thing about learning to read?

_____

What would you do if you were going to help someone learn to read?

_____

Book title _____

Strengths we discussed _____

Progress we discussed _____

Problems we discussed _____

Child concerns _____

Teacher suggestions _____

# Student Self-Assessment

## by Dr. Roger C. Farr

Students need to engage in continuous self-assessment of what they are doing as they construct meaning in reading and writing. This is not just a "How am I doing?" or "How good am I?" kind of evaluation. Rather, it is a matter of determining "*What am I doing? What do I like doing? What do I want to achieve?*"

The procedures students can follow for self-assessment include keeping simple records, writing memos and self-reflection papers about portfolio materials, making notes with the teacher during joint assessment conferences and at other times, and organizing and reorganizing the collection.

■■■■■■■■■■■■■■■■■■■■■■■■■■■■■■

> ## It is a matter of determining "*What am I doing? What do I like doing? What do I want to achieve?*"

Students also need to look at the products they have collected in their portfolios: responses to reading, written expressions, records of how the collection grew, and records of their prior examinations. From this kind of assessment—comparative evaluations of the products over time—the student can draw conclusions about his or her progress. The emphasis is on creating a feeling of success and on encouraging reflection. The student can give substance to this evaluation by writing a story or drawing a picture that represents his or her reading and writing. The evaluation can also be promoted with a letter or memo written to the student's family describing the progress the student sees in the products.

Working with portfolios must become a regular classroom activity that relates to the reading and writing that your students are doing—if the system is to succeed. Time needs to be set aside *regularly,* if not daily, for your students to take out their portfolios and work with them. Portfolio work should not stand apart from classroom instruction. Furthermore, for authentic self-evaluation, the students must be able to *select* products to include in their portfolios.

Name _____

|  | YES | SOMETIMES | NO |
|---|---|---|---|
| **1.** I look at the cover and think of what the story will be about. | ☐ | ☐ | ☐ |
| **2.** I use the pictures to help me understand the story. | ☐ | ☐ | ☐ |
| **3.** I can see in my mind what I am reading about. | ☐ | ☐ | ☐ |
| **4.** I think about what may happen next in the story. | ☐ | ☐ | ☐ |
| **5.** I go back and read things again when they don't make sense. | ☐ | ☐ | ☐ |

**6.** When I come to a word I don't know, I _____

_____

**7.** When I get to the end of a story, I sometimes _____

_____

**On the back is a picture from my favorite story.**

Name _____

|  | YES | SOMETIMES | NO |
|---|---|---|---|
| **1.** I think about what I want to write | ☐ | ☐ | ☐ |
| **2.** I can see in my mind what I am writing about. | ☐ | ☐ | ☐ |
| **3.** When I write, I think about who will read my writing. | ☐ | ☐ | ☐ |
| **4.** I read over my writing to make it better. | ☐ | ☐ | ☐ |
| **5.** I share my work with a classmate. | ☐ | ☐ | ☐ |

**6.** I will draw a line around the things that I like to write.

story          poem          report          note

**7.** Something I do well as a writer is _____

_____

© Harcourt

# PEER ASSESSMENT

## BY DR. ROGER C. FARR

As students develop an increasing awareness of themselves as self-assessors, they become more interested in discussing their development with classmates, who can serve as excellent and highly effective observers. Much of your students' language use, after all, is directed toward their peers; and when it is directed toward some other audience, a student knows that classmates are the first to understand what he or she hopes to accomplish with it.

Students do not always agree about what reading is the most interesting, informative, and valuable; nor do they always agree on the best way to present a written or oral message to other students, the teacher, parents, or other adults.

The opinions of classmates are often highly valued and are sometimes more valued than those of adults; but it is often up to the teacher to encourage collaborative exchange. There are numerous ways to encourage such peer interaction. Here are just a few examples:

- Getting students to share and discuss reactions to reading and to things that their peers write can be as simple as scheduling time during portfolio sessions. Students may choose their own peer partners. You may need to help some students find classmates with whom to share their work. And you may need to model the kind of interaction you hope to achieve with such sessions.
- Many teachers have students work with partners for such exchanges on a regular basis. Some teachers pattern these exchanges on student-teacher conferences.

- A wider sample of peer responses can be achieved by having students give reports to the class—on texts that they have enjoyed reading, for example.
- One of the most effective ways to involve peer reaction is with *classroom publications*. Have students submit favorite pieces of writing (about something they have read, for example), or encourage them to write articles for a classroom newsletter.
- For classes in which students are collecting writing for portfolios, you can provide sheets for peer reaction to pieces in the portfolio.

Conferences with parents or guardians are an important opportunity to share information as well as to learn more about the children we are teaching. It is one of the best times to open communication with parents and to make a positive impression. Teachers have different styles of conferencing, and most are perfectly legitimate. Below are ten simple guidelines to help make conferences more successful.

***Be prepared.*** Have the child's work or portfolio readily accessible. Before the conference, make notes of what you wish to share with the parents. After introductory remarks, begin the conference process. During or after the conference, *immediately* write down what was said. This will help prepare you for the next conference and also document the discussion.

***Provide examples.*** Parents like to see examples of their child's work. Provide some of the best examples first. Parents also like to see growth and improvement. You will probably want to show an example of the child's writing from early in the school year to compare with a more recent effort.

***Discuss strengths first.*** Parents need and deserve to hear what their child does well. Let parents know that you focus on strengths. Later you can discuss concerns or opportunities for growth. As a general rule, discuss at least three strengths before addressing any areas of concern.

***Avoid jargon.*** Speak in a language parents can understand. If you use technical terms, define them briefly. Terms such as metacognition, invented spelling, or K-W-L require an explanation.

***Be realistic.*** Don't promise something that might not happen during the time a child is in your classroom. If he or she is having trouble, address the issue and talk about *reasonable* expectations. Be optimistic, but realistic. It will save you from parental disappointment later on.

# 10 GUIDELINES for a SUCCESSFUL PARENT-TEACHER CONFERENCE

## by Dr. Timothy Rasinski

Professor of Education,
Department of Teaching Leadership and
Curriculum Studies at Kent State University, Ohio.

**Be proactive rather than reactive.**
Inform parents about what the class will be doing during the year and what the specific areas of focus will be. For example, if you're a first-grade teacher using invented spelling, inform parents of the stages or phases they can expect to see in their child's writing in the coming months. If you suspect that many parents may be unfamiliar with or uncertain about an approach you're taking, prepare them for it in advance rather than waiting to hear from them.

**Establish joint responsibility.** Use terms such as "what *we* can do," "*our* focus," etc. Talk specifically about how parents can help you and what you intend to do to help them. For example, "If you will continue to read to Brad each night and be sure he sees you reading . . . ."

**Establish goals, outcomes, and responsibilities.** Tell parents what you plan to do to help their child reach a goal. Then work with them to outline what their responsibilities will be toward that goal. Be sure to discuss the child's responsibilities, too, because you and the family members must be consistent. When children get mixed messages from parents and teachers, they become confused or they may take advantage of the situation.

**Invite questions and information.**
Always ask parents if they have questions about what is occurring in school or why activities are done in a certain way. Encourage parents to share insights into their child's attitudes and behaviors, particularly regarding school. Reassure the parents of children who are having a difficult time personally— a friend has moved away, a pet has died, a family member is ill, etc. Knowledge of these events will be helpful to you.

**Promise to be accessible.** Invite parents to call or leave a message when they have questions or observations. Give them a time when you like to take calls. Encourage them to be involved in school events and to stay in contact with you. Help parents understand that you want their child's school experience to be a rich and rewarding one just as much as they do.

# Home, Community, and School Interaction

## by Dr. Alma Flor Ada

Professor and Director of the Center
for Multicultural Literature for
Children and Young Adults
University of San Francisco

**Children benefit when they experience
understanding between the world of
their home and community and the
world of school. When these two con-
verge, rather than diverge, children
have an opportunity to feel whole.**

Parents benefit from understanding the
goals and purposes of the school, knowing
their child's teacher, and being able to share
concerns and ideas.

Teachers who bring about interaction
between school, home, and community are
able to give added meaning to their curriculum and to make their classes more relevant for children. As a first step in creating
permanent ties between home, community,
and school, teachers can ask themselves
some basic questions.

**For example:**

**?** **What strategies am I developing to ensure the growth of each child's first language (whether I can speak that language or not) as the vehicle for home interaction?**

**?** **In what ways am I incorporating parents' lives, experiences, and their information and ability to construct knowledge into the school lives of their children?**

**?** **How can I foster communication at home between parents and children?**

**?** **What am I doing to use the printed word as a means of validating and celebrating parents?**

**?** **Are there different ways to encourage parents and children to act as agents of their own liberation?**

As every teacher reflects upon these questions and provides responses based on his or her individual experience, a body of strategies will develop and may be shared within each school among teachers at all levels.

Parent participation can take many forms. This article focuses on participation that takes place on a daily basis and that doesn't necessarily require parents to be physically present in the school. These suggestions may serve as a starting point for sharing among teachers in each educational community.

1. **Encourage children to return home daily with something to share with their parents.** Children might ask a question about a topic they discussed in school that day or share news about a classroom project.

2. **Facilitate interviews of parents by their children.** If the information requested from parents encourages them to revisit their own childhoods, they may in the process develop a greater understanding of their own children. The sharing of childhood memories with their children not only provides a

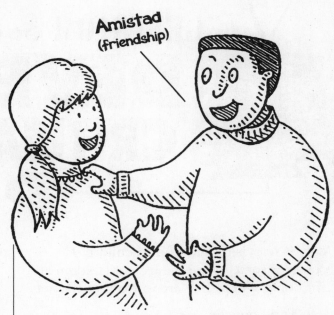

Amistad (friendship)

framework for communication but also promotes better parenting.

3. **Expand whole-language activities outside the classroom.** Just as you ask children to predict the content of a book you are going to read to them—from the title and cover illustration, from names of the characters, or from the first paragraph—you can ask children to invite their parents to offer similar predictions.

4. **Engage children in retelling a story to their parents and then having them ask their parents for a sequel.**

5. **Ask parents to participate in classroom discussions.** For example, if you have discussed the topic of friendship, ask children to interview their parents about childhood friends or about the kinds of games they played or about the ways they resolved conflicts. Children can also learn from their parents how to say *friendship* in the home language and then bring the word back to share with the class.

6. **Children can author books in which they are the protagonists, using information they have obtained from their parents.** For example, they might write about *How I got my name, My autobiography,* or *Something big that happened when I was little.* 🍎

# TELEVISION & CHILDREN: DEVELOPING CRITICAL THINKING

## BY JUDY GIGLIO

Why is television harmful to children? Consider some of the things that children are *not* doing when they are in front of the set:

playing outside
reading
having a conversation
solving problems
asking questions
using their imagination
interacting with the real world
homework or family chores

If most parents are unwilling or unable to limit television in their homes, what can teachers do? They can work with parents to help children develop good viewing habits. Parents *can* teach their children to be selective viewers who use good judgment when tuning in shows.

### Description of a TV-Wise Child

- selects programs for good reasons
- spends a limited number of hours viewing TV
- appreciates shows that are well done
- recognizes shows that are poorly done
- knows he or she can ask questions before, during, and after a show

Children will not be able to make smart choices about television all by themselves. They need your help and help from family members. Early in the school year or when you do a family or neighborhood theme, plan to spend some class time talking to children about their television-watching

habits. As a follow-up, send home the copying master on page 165. It is designed to

- let parents know you're concerned about children's TV-viewing habits
- make parents aware of their own viewing habits
- offer suggestions for judging the shows children watch
- offer suggestions for home activities that emphasize the positive aspects of television viewing

> "Television is the school's primary competitor for children's minds."
>
> **Jim Trelease**
> *The Read-Aloud Handbook*

Family members, are you setting an example for children of how to view television wisely? Here is a checklist for you.

**YES**    **NO**

_____  _____    I often watch the shows my child selects.

_____  _____    My child shares ideas prompted by TV viewing.

_____  _____    My child uses good judgment when selecting shows.

_____  _____    Topics from TV shows often motivate my child to read books for additional information.

_____  _____    I limit the amount of time I view television.

_____  _____    I help my child evaluate the shows he or she watches.

_____  _____    If I object to a show, I explain why to my child.

- If you responded **YES** to every question, you are a **TV-wise parent!**

**TV REPORT CARD FOR FAMILY MEMBERS**

Watch the shows your children watch. Answer these questions as you watch.

**YES**    **NO**

_____  _____    Is this show appropriate for my child's age?

_____  _____    Is the program free of content that might frighten or disturb my child?

_____  _____    Is the program free of violence?

_____  _____    Does the program omit stereotyping of a particular gender, race, or ethnic group?

_____  _____    Does the program offer content that will enhance learning or stimulate my child's imagination?

**TV-wise Parents:** *Remember, you control the on/off knob! With courage and determination, you can limit television's influence on your children.*

# PROFESSIONAL BOOKSHELF

**Adams, M.J.** (1990). *Beginning to Read: Thinking and Learning About Print.* Cambridge, MA: MIT Press.

**Allington, R.L. & Cunningham, P.M.** (1996). *Schools That Work.* Reading, MA: Addison-Wesley.

**Allington, R.L. & Cunningham, P.M.** (1999). *Classrooms That Work: They Can All Read and Write.* (Second Edition). MA: Addison-Wesley.

**Altieri, D.** (1991). At-risk students: Consider integrated strategies. *Education Canada, 31(3),* 24–26.

**Anderson, P., & Rubano, G.** (1991). *Enhancing Aesthetic Reading and Response. Theory and Research Into Practice (TRIP Series).* Urbana, IL: NCTE.

**Anderson, R., & Others.** (1988). Growth in reading and how children spend their time outside of school. *Reading Research Quarterly,* 23(3), 285–303.

**Anderson, R., & Others.** (Eds.). (1985). *Becoming a Nation of Readers: The Report of the Commission on Reading.* Illinois University, Urbana, IL: Center for the Study of Reading.

**Arter, J.A.** (1992). NCME Instructional Module: Using portfolios of student work in instruction and assessment. *Educational Measurement: Issues and Practice,* 11(1), 36–44.

**Asher, J.** (1977). *Learning Another Language Through Actions.* Los Gatos, CA: Sky Oaks Productions.

**Atwell, N.** (1987). *In the Middle: Writing, Reading and Learning with Adolescents.* Portsmouth, NH: Heinemann.

**Banks, J.A., & Banks, C.M.** (Eds.). (1989). *Multicultural Education: Issues and Perspectives.* Needham Heights, MA: Simon & Schuster.

**Bear, D.** (1992). The Prosody of Oral Reading and Stages of Word Knowledge. In S. Templeton & D. Bear (Eds.) *Development of Orthographic Knowledge and the Foundations of Literacy: A Memorial Festschrift for Edmund H. Henderson.* Mahwah, NJ: Lawrence Erlbaum.

**Bear, D.R., Invernizzi, M., & Templeton, S.** (1996). *Words Their Way: Word Study for Phonics, Vocabulary, and Spelling Instruction.* Englewood Cliffs, NJ: Prentice Hall.

**Beck, I.L., & Juel, C.** (1992). The role of decoding in learning to read. *What Research Has To Say about Reading Instruction.* Newark, DE: International Reading Association.

**Berghoff, B., & Egawa, K.** (1991). No more "rocks": Grouping to give students control of their learning. *The Reading Teacher,* 44(8), 536–541.

**Bredekamp, S. & Copple, C.** (Ed.). (1997). *Developmentally Appropriate Practice in Early Childhood.* (Revised Edition). Washington, DC: NAEYC.

**Butler, A., & Turbill, J.** (1984). *Towards a Reading-Writing Classroom.* Primary English Teaching Association. New South Whales: Australia.

**Byrum, D., & Pierce, V.L.** (1993). *Bringing children to literacy through theme cycles. In Harp, Bill (Ed.) Bringing Children to Literacy: Classrooms at Work.* Norwood, MA: Christopher-Gordon.

**Caine, R.N., & Caine, G.** (1991). *Making Connections: Teaching and the Human Brain.* Alexandria, VA: ASCD.

**Calkins, L.M.** (1986). *The Art of Teaching Writing.* Portsmouth, NH: Heinemann.

**Calkins, L.M.** (1990). *Living Between the Lines.* Portsmouth, NH: Heinemann.

**Cambourne, B.** (1993). *The Whole Story: Natural Learning and the Acquisition of Literacy in the Classroom.* New York: Scholastic.

**Carbo, M.** (1997). *How to Record Books for Maximum Reading Gains.* (Third Edition). Syosset, NY: National Reading Styles Institute.

**Cavarretta, J.** (1998). Parents are a school's best friend. *Educational Leadership,* 55(8), 12–15.

**Chapman, C.** (1993). *If the Shoe Fits…How to Develop Multiple Intelligences in the Classroom.* Arlington Heights, IL: Skylight.

**Chatton, B.** (1993). *Using Poetry Across the Curriculum: A Whole Language Approach.* Phoenix, AZ: Oryx Press.

**Clay, M.** (1993). *An Observation Survey: Of Early Literacy Achievement.* Portsmouth, NH: Heinemann.

**Clay, M.** (1993). *Reading Recovery: A Guidebook for Teachers in Training.* Portsmouth, NH: Heinemann.

**Clymer, T.** (1996). The utility of phonic generalizations in the primary grades. *The Reading Teacher,* 16(4), 252–258.

**Cole, R.W.** (Ed.). (1995). *Educating Everybody's Children: Diverse Teaching Strategies for Diverse Learners: What Research Has to Say About Improving Achievement.* Alexandria, VA: ASCD.

**Costa, A.** (1984). Mediating the metacognitive. *Educational Leadership,* 42(3), 57.

**Crafton, L.** (1994). *Challenges of Holistic Teaching: Answering the Tough Questions.* Norwood, MA: Christopher-Gordon.

**Cullinan, B.E. & Galda, L.** (1994). *Literature and the Child.* (Third Edition). Fort Worth, TX: Harcourt Brace.

**Cullinan, B.E.** (Ed.). (1987). *Children's Literature in the Reading Program.* Newark, DE: IRA.

**Cullinan, B.E.** (Ed.). (1992). *Invitation to Read: More Children's Literature in the Reading Program.* Newark, DE: International Reading Association.

**Cullinan, B.E.**, Scala, M. & Schroder, V. (1995). *Three Voices: A Guide to Poetry Across the Curricu-lum.* York, ME: Stenhouse.

**Cunningham, P.M. & Cunningham, J.W.** (1992). Making words: Enhancing the invented spelling-decoding connection. *The Reading Teacher,* 46(2), 106–115.

**Cunningham, P.M.** (1990). *Phonics They Use.* Reading, MA: Addison-Wesley.

**Dakos, K.** (1990). *If You're Not Here, Please Raise Your Hand: Poems About School.* New York: Simon & Schuster.

**Davies, A., Politano, C., & Cameron, C.** (1993). *Making Themes Work.* Grand Forks, ND: Pegasis.

**Dole, J.A. & Others.** (1991). Moving from the old to the new: Research on reading comprehension instruction. *Review of Educational Research,* 61(2), 239–264.

**Duffy, G., & Roehler, L.** (1993). *Improving Classroom Reading Instruction: A Decison-Making Approach.* (Third Edition). New York: McGraw-Hill.

**Dyrli, O.E., & Kinnaman, D.E.** (1994). Gaining access to technology: First step in making a difference for your students. *Technology and Learning,* 14(4), 15–20, 48, 50.

**Dyrli, O.E., & Kinnaman, D.E.** (1994). The online connection: Plunging into cyberspace. *Technology and Learning,* 16(1), 24.

**Dyson, A.H.** (1982). Reading, writing, and language: Young children solving the written language puzzle. *Language Arts,* 59(8), 829–839.

**Eller, R.G., & Others.** (1988). The lexical development of kindergartners: Learning from written context. *Journal of Reading Behavior,* 20(1), 5–24.

**Elley, W.B.** (1989). Vocabulary acquistion from listening to stories. *Reading Research Quarterly,* 24(2), 174–187.

**Evertson, C.M., & Harris, A.H.** (1992). What we know about managing classrooms. *Educational Leadership,* 49(7), 74–78.

**Fagan, W.T.** (1989). Empowered students; empowered teachers, *The Reading Teacher,* 42(8), 572–578.

**Farr, R. & Tone, B.** (1998). *Portfolio and Performance Assessment: Helping Students Evaluate Their Progress as Readers and Writers.* (Second Edition). Austin, TX: Harcourt Brace.

**Farr, R.** (1990). Setting directions for language arts portfolios. *Educational Leadership,* 48(3), 103.

**Farr, R.** (1992). Putting it all together: Solving the reading assessment puzzle. (Distinguished Educator Series). *The Reading Teacher,* 46(1), 26–37.

**Fielding, L.G., & Pearson, P.D.** (1994). Reading comprehension: What works. *Educational Leadership,* 51(5), 62–68.

**Flood, J., & Lapp, D.** (1989). Reporting reading progess: A comparison portfolio for parents. *The Reading Teacher,* 42(7), 508–514.

**Flores, B., & Others.** (1991). Transforming deficit myths about learning, language, and culture. *Language Arts,* 68(5), 369–379.

**Fogarty, R.** (1991). Ten ways to integrate curriculum. *Educational Leadership,* 49(2), 61–65.

**Fox, Barbara J.** (1995). *Strategies for Word Identification: Phonics from a New Perspective.* Englewood Cliffs, NJ: Prentice-Hall.

**Frazier, D.M. & Paulson, F.L.** (1992). How portfolios motivate reluctant writers. *Educational Leadership.* 49(8), 62–65.

**Fredericks, A., & Others.** (1997). *Thematic Units: An Integrated Approach Teaching Science and Social Studies.* Reading, MA: Addison-Wesley.

**Freppon, P.A., & Dahl, K.L.** (1991). Learning about phonics in a whole-language classroom. *Language Arts,* 68(3), 190–197.

**Gardner, H.** (1993). *Frames of Mind: The Theory of Multiple Intelligences.* (Second Edition). New York: Basic Books.

**Gentry, J.R.** (1989). *Spel Is a Four-Letter Word.* Portsmouth, NH: Heinemann.

**Gold, R.** (1997). K-W-L: A Strategy for Active Reading. *English Teacher's Journal* (Israel). 51, 62–66.

**Goodman, Y.M.** (1989). Evaluation of Students. In K.S. Goodman, Y.M. Goodman, and W. Hood (Eds.) *The Whole Language Evaluation Book.* Portsmouth, NH: Heinemann.

**Goodman, Y.M.** (Ed.). (1990). *How Children Construct Literacy: Piagetian Perspectives.* Newark, DE: International Reading Association.

**Graves, D.** (1989). *Writing: Teachers and Children at Work.* Portsmouth, NH: Heinemann.

**Gunning, T.G.** (1995). Word building: A strategic approach to the teaching of phonics. *The Reading Teacher,* 48(6), 484–488.

**Hansen, J.** (1992). Literacy portfolios emerge. *The Reading Teacher,* 45(8), 604–607.

**Harp, B.** (1989). How are we using what we know about literacy processes in the content areas? *The Reading Teacher,* 42(7), 726–727.

**Harris, J.** (1995). Mining the Internet: Making the Hypertext happen: HTML commands in NCSA's *Mosaic. Computing Teacher,* 22(4), 36–41.

**Harris, J.** (1995). *Way of the Ferret: Finding and Using Educational Resources on the Internet.* Eugene, OR: ISTE.

**Harste, J.C., & Short, K.G., with Burke, C.** (1988). *Creating Classrooms for Authors: The Reading-Writing Connection.* Portsmouth, NH: Heinemann.

**Harwayne, S.** (1993). *Lasting Impressions: Weaving Literature into the Writing Workshop.* Portsmouth, NH: Heinemann.

**Hilliard, A.G., III.** (1991). Do we have the will to educate all children? *Educational Leadership,* 49(1), 31–36.

**Hilliard, A.G., III.** (1991). Why we must pluralize the curriculum. *Educational Leadership,* 49(4), 12–16.

**Hopkins, L.B.** (1998). *Pass the Poetry, Please!* (Third Edition). New York: HarperCollins.

Hornsby, D., & Others. (1988). *Read on: A Conference Approach to Reading.* Portsmouth, NH: Heinemann.

Hoyt, L. (1992). Many ways of knowing: Using drama, oral interactions, and the visual arts to enhance reading comprehension. *The Reading Teacher,* 45(8), 580-584.

Johns, J.L. (1991). Helping readers at risk: Beyond whole language, whole word, and phonics. *International Journal of Reading, Writing, and Learning Disabilities,* 7(1), 59-67.

Johnson, D.W., Johnson, R.T., & Holubec, E.J. (1994). *The New Circles of Learning: Cooperation in the Classroom and School.* Alexandria, VA: ASCD.

Karolides, N.J. (Ed.). (1997). *Reader Response in the Classroom: Evoking & Interpreting Meaning in Literature.* Mahwah, NJ: Lawrence Erlbaum.

Kasten, W.C., & Clarke, B.K. (1993). *The Multi-age Classroom—A Family of Learners.* Katonah, NY: Owen.

Kidder, T. (1990). *Among Schoolchildren.* New York: Avon.

Krashen, S. (1989). We acquire vocabulary and spelling by reading: Additional evidence for the Input Hypothesis. *Modern Language Journal,* 73(4) 440-464.

Krashen, S. (1993). *The Power of Reading: Insights from the Research.* Englewood, CO: Libraries Unlimited.

Krashen, S. (1994). Some new evidence for an old hypothesis. In J. Alatis (Ed.) *Georgetown University Round Table on Languages and Linguistics.* Washington, DC: Georgetown University Press. 413-427.

Langer, J. A. (Ed.). (1992). *Literature Instruction:* A Focus on Student Response. Urbana, IL: NCTE.

Larrick, N. (1991). *Let's Do a Poem: Introducing Poetry to Children.* New York: Delacorte.

Lazear, D. (1991). *Seven Ways of Teaching: The Artistry of Teaching with Multiple Intelligences.* Arlington Heights, IL: Skylight.

Leonhardt, M. (1995). *Parents Who Love Reading, Kids Who Don't.* New York: Crown.

Lindgren, M. (1991). *The Multicolored Mirror: Cultural Substance in Literature for Children and Young Adults.* Fort Atkinson, WI: Highsmith Press.

Manning, G.L., & Manning, M. (1984). What models of recreational reading make a difference? *Reading World,* 23(4), 375-380.

Marzano, R. J., et al. (1988). *Dimensions of Thinking: A Framework for Curriculum & Instruction.* Alexandria, VA: ASCD.

McCarrier, A. & Others. (2000). *Interactive Writing: How Language & Literacy Come Together, K-2,* Portsmouth, NH. Heinemann.

McCarthy, B. (1985). What 4Mat training teaches us about staff development. *Educational Leadership,* 42(7), 61-68.

Michel, P.A. (1994). *The Child's View of Reading: Understandings for Teachers and Parents.* Needham Heights, MA: Allyn and Bacon.

Mooney, M. (1991). *Developing Life-Long Readers.* New York: Richard C. Owens.

Nagy, W. & Herman, P. (1987). Breadth and depth of vocabulary knowledge: Implications for acquisition and instruction. In M. McKeown & M. Curtis (Eds.) *The Nature of Vocabulary Acquisition.* Mawah, NJ: Lawrence Erlbaum. 19-35.

Nagy, W.E., & Others. (1985). Learning words from context. *Reading Research Quarterly,* 20(2), 233-253.

Neill, S.B., & Neill, G.W. *Only the Best: Annual Guide to the Highest-Rated Education Software—Multimedia for Preschool-Grade 12.* Education News Service.

Norton, D.E. (1990). Teaching multicultural literature in the reading curriculum. *The Reading Teacher,* 44(1), 28-40.

Ogle, D. (1986). K-W-L: A teaching model that develops active reading of expository text. *The Reading Teacher,* 39(6), 564-570.

Pappas, C. C., & Others. (1995). *An Integrated Language Perspective in the Elementary School: Theory into Action.* White Plains, NY: Longman.

Pellowski, A. (1990). *The World of Storytelling: A Practical Guide to the Origins, Development, and Application of Storytelling.* (Second Edition). New York: H.W. Wilson.

Pikulski, J. (1994). Preventing reading failure: A review of five effective programs. *The Reading Teacher,* 48, 30-39.

Pinnell, G.S. & Fountas, I.C. (1998). *Word Matters: Teaching Phonics and Spelling in the Reading/Writing Classroom. A Companion Volume to Guided Reading.* Portsmouth, NH: Heinemann

Pitts, M., & Others. (1989). Acquiring second language vocabulary through reading: A replication of the Clockwork Orange study using second language acquirers. *Reading in a Foreign Language,* 5(2), 271-275.

Pope, C.A. & Kutiper, K. (1988). Using magazines in the English classroom. *English Journal,* 77(8), 66-68.

Preece, A., & Cowden, D. (1993). *Young Writers in the Making: Sharing the Process with Parents.* Portsmouth, NH: Heinemann.

Purves, A., et al. (1998). *How Porcupines Make Love.* (Fourth Edition). Reading, MA: Addison-Wesley.

Radencich, M.C., & McKay, L.J. (1995). *Flexible Grouping for Literacy in the Elementary Grades.* Needham Heights: Allyn & Bacon.

Rasinski, T. (1989). Reading and the empowerment of parents. *The Reading Teacher,* 43(3), 226-231.

Rasinski, T. (1994). *Parents, Teachers, and Literacy Learning.* Fort Worth, TX: Harcourt Brace.

Read, C. (1975). *Children's Categorization of Speech Sounds in English.* Urbana, IL: NCTE.

Reutzel, D.R., & Fawson, P. (1990). Traveling tales: Connecting parents and children through writing. *The Reading Teacher,* 44(3), 222-227.

**Rigg, P., & Allen, V.G.** (1989). *When They Don't All Speak English: Integrating the ESL Student into the Regular Classroom.* Urbana, IL: NCTE.

**Rosenblatt, L. M.** (1983). *Literature as Exploration.* Fourth ed. New York: Modern Language Association of America.

**Rosenblatt, L.M.** (1994). *The Reader, the Text, the Poem: The Transactional Theory of the Literary Work.* Carbondale, IL: Southern Illnois University Press.

**Routman, R. (1994).** *Invitations: Changing as Teachers and Learners K-12.* Portsmouth, NH: Heinemann.

**Royer, J.M., & Carlo, M.S.** (1991). Transfer of comprehension skills from native to second language. *Journal of Reading,* 34(6), 450-455.

**Samuels, S.J.** (1988). Decoding and automaticity: Helping poor readers become automatic at word recognition. *The Reading Teacher,* 41(8), 756-760.

**Schwartz, R., & Raphael, T.E.** (1985). Concept of definition: A key to improving students' vocabulary. *The Reading Teacher,* 39(2), 198-205.

**Short, K.G., & Pierce, K.M.** (1998). *Talking About Books: Creating Literate Communities.* Portsmouth, NH: Heinemann.

**Slavin, R.E., et al.** (1988). Accommodating student diversity in reading and writing instruction: A cooperative learning approach. *Remedial and Special Education,* 9(1), 60-66.

**Snow, C. & Ferguson, C.** (Eds.) (1979). Talking to Children. New York: Cambridge University Press.

**Snow, C.E. & Others** (Eds.) (1998). *Preventing Reading Difficulties in Young Children.* National Academy of Sciences—National Research Council, Washington DC Commission on Behavioral and Social Sciences and Education.

**Spiegel, D.** (1995). A comparison of traditional remedial programs and Reading Recovery: Guidelines for success for all programs. *The Reading Teacher,* 49(2), 86-96.

**Stahl, S.A & Others.** (1990). *Beginning to Read: Thinking and Learning About Print—A Summary.* Champaign, IL: Center for the Study of Reading, University of Illinois at Urbana-Champaign.

**Strickland, D. S.** (1998). *Teaching Phonics Today: A Primer for Educators.* Newark, DE: IRA.

**Strickland, D. S.** (1995). Reinventing our literacy programs: Books, basics, balance. *The Reading Teacher,* 48(4), 294-302.

**Strickland, D. S., & Morrow, L.** (1989). Creating curriculum: An emergent literacy perspective. *The Reading Teacher,* 42(9), 722-723.

**Strickland, D. S., & Morrow, L.** (Eds.). (1989). *Emerging Literacy: Young Children Learn to Read and Write.* Newark, DE: IRA.

**Taylor, D.** (1995). *Family Literacy.* (Second Edition). Portsmouth, NH: Heinemann.

**Taylor, D., & Dorsey-Gaines, C.** (1988). *Growing Up Literate: Learning from Inner-City Families.* Portsmouth, NH: Heinemann.

**Trachtenburg, P.** (1990). Using children's literature to enhance phonics instruction. *The Reading Teacher,* 43(9), 648-654.

**Trachtenburg, P., & Ferruggia, A.** (1989). Big books from little voices: Reaching high-risk beginning readers. *The Reading Teacher,* 42(4), 284-289.

**Trelease, J.** (1995). *The Read-Aloud Handbook.* New York: Viking.

**Truett, C.** (1994). The Internet: What's in it for me? *The Computing Teacher,* 22(3), 66-68.

**Tunnell, M.O., & Jacobs, J.S.** (1989). Using "real" books: Research findings on literature-based reading instruction. *The Reading Teacher,* 42(7), 470-477.

**Wepner, S.B.** (1991). Technology-based literature plans for elementary students. *The Reading Teacher,* 45(3), 236-238.

**Wepner, S.B., & Seminoff, N.E.** (1994). Saving endangered species: *Using technology to teach thematically. The Computing Teacher,* 22(1), 34-37.

**Wepner, S.B., Strickland, D. S., & Feely, J.** (1987). *Using Computers in the Teaching of Reading.* New York: Teachers College Press.

**Werner, P.H.** (1992). Integrated assessment system. *Journal of Reading,* 35(5), 416-418.

**Wilde, S.** (1997). *What's a Schwa Sound Anyway?: A Holistic Guide to Phonetics, Phonics, and Spelling.* Portsmouth, NH. Heinemann.

**Wilde, S.** (1992). *You Kan Red This!: Spelling and Punctuation for Whole Language Classrooms,* K-6. Portsmouth, NH: Heinemann.

**Yancy, K.B.** (Ed.). (1992). *Portfolios in the Writing Classroom: An Introduction.* Urbana, IL: NCTE.

**Yokota, J.** (1993). Issues in selecting multicultural children's literature. *Language Arts,* 70(3), 156-167.

**Yopp, H.K.** (1992). Developing phonemic awareness in young children. *The Reading Teacher,* 45(9), 696-703.

**Yopp, H.K.** (1995). A test for assessing phonemic awareness in young children. *The Reading Teacher,* 49(1), 20-29.

**Yopp, H.K.** (1995). Read-aloud books for developing phonemic awareness: An annotated bibliography. *The Reading Teacher,* 48(6), 538-542.

© Harcourt

# GLOSSARY OF PROFESSIONAL TERMS

**AFFECTIVE RESPONSE** A response that expresses emotions or feelings and goes beyond literal detail.

**ALPHABETIC PRINCIPLE** There is a relationship between spoken sounds and individual letters or combinations of letters.

**ANALYTIC LEARNERS** Tend to be highly logical, rational, organized, detail-oriented; enjoy highly organized teaching.

**ANTICIPATION GUIDE** A comprehension strategy for nonfiction in which the teacher provides several topic-related statements and students use prior knowledge to tell whether the statements are true or false; students return to the statements after reading and revise their responses.

**AUDITORY ACTIVITY** An activity in which students identify and differentiate sounds, rhyming words, and word patterns; an activity in which learning is promoted through the sense of hearing.

**AUDITORY LEARNERS** Learn by listening and speaking; recall what they hear; enjoy discussions.

**AUTHOR'S CHAIR** A special chair in which a student author sits to read his/her writing for response from a group or from the class.

**BALANCED INSTRUCTION** An instructional program that balances the emphasis on helping children acquire relevant skills and knowledge with an emphasis on helping them learn to use those skills and knowledge in independent, productive, and thoughtful reading and writing.

**BRAIN-BASED LEARNING** A term used to describe how brain-research findings are applied to the classroom environment—using what is known about how learning happens in the brain helps to provide stimulating classroom environments.

**BRAINSTORMING** Expressing ideas without stopping to evaluate them; searching for ideas or solutions through group discussion; a prewriting strategy.

**CHORAL READING** Reading verse or patterned language in groups by alternating lines or passages.

**COMMUNITY OF READERS** A classroom in which students have an integral part in defining roles, routines, and rules and have a sense that reading is a worthwhile, meaningful experience that should be shared.

**COOPERATIVE LEARNING** Working in pairs or small groups to accomplish goals and generate products interdependently; students may be assigned specific roles, such as Reader, Recorder, and Reporter.

**CREATIVE DRAMATICS** Informally acting out a story or a poem; responding to literature through drama.

**CREATIVE THINKING** Generating and expressing thoughts imaginatively, uniquely, or poetically through relational patterns of language and thought; thought processes characterized by problem identification, hypothesis formation, and solution evaluation.

**CRITICAL THINKING** Making judgments about the validity, quality, and accuracy of ideas or text; judging the qualifications of an author or the actions and traits of a character; logical analysis and judgment of worth based on sound criteria.

**CULMINATING LEARNING EXPERIENCES** Activities designed to allow learners to summarize, synthesize, and share their new learning; these experiences often have a feeling of celebration. Students may also decide what else they would like to investigate related to a theme or topic.

**DIALOGUING** Talking in pairs or small groups; carrying on a written or spoken dialogue with another person; specifically, ongoing written conversation between a teacher and an individual student, often in a journal.

**DECODABLE TEXT** Decodable text is connected text composed of words that use the sound-spelling correspondences that children have learned to that point and a limited number of sight words that have been systematically taught.

© Harcourt

**ECHO READING**   A form of reading in which students repeat phrases after the teacher.

**EXPLICIT INSTRUCTION**   The practice of demonstrating and bringing to learners' conscious awareness those convert and invisible processes, understandings, knowledge, and skills necessary for effective reading.

**FLEXIBLE GROUPING**   Temporary grouping that varies according to instructional goals and students' needs and interests; includes the whole group, teacher-facilitated small groups, cooperative groups, pairs, and individuals.

**FLUENCY**   The ability to read smoothly, without hesitation, and without word-identification problems that might hinder comprehension.

**GLOBAL LEARNERS**   Tend to be strongly intuitive, emotional, group-oriented; highly responsive to holistic teaching.

**GRAPHIC ORGANIZER**   A visual representation that aids meaning; a vehicle for organizing ideas to show relationships among them; webs, charts, and diagrams.

**GRAPHOPHONICS**   The relationships between print and the sounds of spoken language; one part of a cueing system readers use to make sense of text.

**GUIDED READING**   Reading by students in small groups on their instructional level with the teacher acting as facilitator, prompting and assisting each student; an approach where a teacher and a group of students talk, read, and think their way purposefully through a text.

**INFORMAL ASSESSMENT**   Observation of student progress to diagnose student needs; sampling of ability or performance, including portfolios in which representative samples of student work are gathered over time.

**INQUIRY LEARNING**   When students pursue information to answer their own questions about a topic or theme; inquiry learning involves authentic processes of reading, writing, speaking, and listening as students determine sources, read for information, take notes, use information in written products, deliver information, and listen to others deliver information.

**INTEGRATED CURRICULUM**   Combining subject areas in a unified approach; teaching social studies, science, math, language arts, and other content areas as related parts of a whole.

**INTEGRATED LANGUAGE ARTS**   Teaching speaking, listening, reading, and writing as meaning-based, related parts of a whole.

**KID WATCHING**   Informal observation of children as they engage in language activities.

**KINESTHETIC ACTIVITY**   An activity involving physical movement, jumping or walking; an activity in which learning is promoted through large-muscle movement.

**KINESTHETIC LEARNERS**   Learn through whole-body movement; recall what they experience; enjoy acting and direct experience.

**K-W-L**   A learning strategy for reading non-fiction, consisting of listing what you *know,* what you *want* to know, and what you have *learned.*

**K-W-L CHART**   A graphic organizer that allows individual students or groups of students to consider what they know (K), what they want to know (W), ad what they have learned (L); the first two columns are completed before the inquiry for new information begins, and the final column is completed after inquiry.

**LANGUAGE EXPERIENCE**   Using students' own words as a source for reading and learning; for example, having children dictate or retell a story, recording their sentences on the board, then rereading the story and discussing characters, cause and effect, and so on.

**LEARNING STYLES**   Ways in which we learn: visual, auditory, tactile, and kinesthetic are the four most commonly known.

**LITERATURE-BASED**   Characterized by the use of high-quality stories, poems, and non-fiction to teach reading, writing, listening, and speaking; driven by the belief that surrounding children with good literature will help them become lifelong readers and learners.

**LITERATURE CIRCLE**   A group that meets regularly to respond to literature.

**METACOGNITION**   A level of thinking that involves the examination of one's own state of knowledge; awareness of thinking and learning processes; "thinking about thinking."

**MINILESSON**   A brief instructional session provided when a teacher diagnoses a need, in which concepts, skills, or strategies are introduced in a meaningful context through student-teacher interaction.

**MODELING**   A demonstration of behaviors for novices to imitate; "thinking aloud" to make explicit or public what one does or thinks about while reading, writing, listening, or speaking; an element of explicit instruction.

**MULTI-AGE**   Classrooms (sometimes called "nongraded") in which children of several chronological ages are taught together.

**MULTICULTURALISM**   The inclusion, integration, and appreciation of literature, concepts, art, contributions, and values of diverse cultural groups.

**MULTIPLE INTELLIGENCES**   A theory developed by Harvard psychologist Howard Gardner; it asserts that there are a number of human capacities that are not examined by typical I.Q. tests and that these capacities should be recognized and fostered in schools. They are Verbal/Linguistic, Musical/Rhythmic, Logical/Mathematical, Visual/Spatial, Bodily/Kinesthetic, Intrapersonal, Interpersonal, and Naturalist.

**PHONEMIC AWARENESS**   The awareness that the speech stream consists of a series of sounds (phonemes) that can be manipulated.

**PORTFOLIO ASSESSMENT**   Evaluation based on the regular collection of student work samples over a period of time.

**PREVIEWING AND PREDICTING**   A pre-reading strategy that involves looking over a text to infer what it might be about and how it should be read; using knowledge about language and the context in which it occurs to anticipate what is forthcoming in writing or speech.

**READABILITY**   Ease of comprehension; involves variables in text and variables within the reader.

**READER RESPONSE**   The construction of meaning through interaction with text; active and personal participation in reading and responding.

**READERS THEATRE**   A literature response activity in which students translate a narrative or poem into a script and read it aloud; a simply staged performance that requires little preparation.

**READING STYLE**   The application of learning-style theory to the teaching of reading, with implications for reading instruction.

**RECORDED-BOOK METHOD**   A method of recording very small portions of a challenging story at a slow pace to increase students' reading fluency.

**REPEATED READING**   A strategy designed to help students read successfully and fluently. A passage is read *to* students, then read *with* students, and then practiced *by* students until mastered.

**ROLE-PLAY**   Acting out a part in order to understand another's feelings or how to do something.

**SCAFFOLDING**   Supporting a novice learner by modeling dialogue, strategies, and responses and then gradually withdrawing support as the learner becomes increasingly independent.

**SKILL**   An acquired ability to perform well.

**SORTING**   Clustering or categorizing according to some distinguishing feature; strategy for helping students see relationships among spelling words.

**STRATEGY**   A systematic plan for achieving a specific goal or result; an approach to learning that gives students methods for mastering tasks and gaining skills.

**STORY THEATER**   Groups of students each reading parts of a selection while other students pantomime the action.

**TACTILE ACTIVITY**   An activity involving touch, such as tracing sandpaper letters, playing a board game, folding paper; an activity in which learning is promoted through touching and feeling with the hands.

**TACTILE LEARNERS**   Learn by touching; recall what they touch; enjoy games and manipulating objects.

**TEXT SET** A group of related books or selections; texts in the set may have the same author, theme, or topic. Students may read different texts in the set and then meet to explore the connections among them, or each student may read more than one text.

**THEMATIC UNIT** An organizational method for delivering content and promoting process experiences in reading, writing, speaking, and listening. Thematic units can be organized around a common topic, concept, genre, or author. Opportunities for ample experiences with literature, research, cooperative group activities, and choices for exploration are usually present.

**THEME** A central or dominating idea around which reading materials, concepts, and instruction can be organized; a message or idea that dominates a work of literature or art.

**THINK ALONG** A demonstration of behaviors for learners to imitate; "thinking aloud" to make explicit or public what one does or thinks about while reading, writing, listening, or speaking.

**VISUAL ACTIVITY** An activity that involves discrimination among differences in color, shape, and other visual stimuli; an activity in which learning is promoted through sight.

**VISUAL LEARNERS** Learn by observing; recall what they see; notice details; enjoy demonstrations.

**WAIT TIME** A brief period during which the teacher waits for students to respond rather than providing the answer or moving to another question.

**WHOLE LANGUAGE** An instructional approach based on the belief that learning is a social experience and that children learn from complete texts, high-quality literature, integrated instruction, and ongoing practice and experimentation in language use.

**WRITER'S WORKSHOP** A block of time devoted to writing; can include minilessons, prewriting, drafting, responding and revising, proofreading, and publishing; a session that provides time to write, ownership of written products, and other conditions for writing and sharing.

**WRITING PROCESS** A framework for writing in which students use some or all of the following steps: prewriting, drafting, revising and responding, proofreading, and publishing; an approach to writing that allows students to shape and reshape their language over a period of time, not necessarily following a rigid order or number or steps.

# INDEX

© Harcourt

Evaluation
*See* Assessment
**Experience chart, 83**

**Facilitator, teacher as,** 93, 125, 154, 160
**Family involvement,** 20, 64, 67, 74, 78, 80–81, 150, 160–161, 162–163, 164–165
**Farr, Roger C.,** 23, 125, 133, 137, 140, 144, 148, 149, 156, 159
**Fiction,** 103, 104, 105
**Flexible grouping,** 9, 11–14
*See also* Groups and Classroom management
**Fluency,** 28, 32, 51, 68
**Formal assessment,** 10, 43, 121–122, 126
**Formal language,** 73
**Free reading,** 74–76, 112–114, 122

**Gallego, Margaret A.,** 40
**Genre,** 37, 99–100, 101, 106
**Gerhart, Lorraine,** 11
**Gifted and talented,** 49, 69–71
**Giglio, Judy,** 164
**Grammar**
*See* Nonstandard English; Responding and revising
**Graphic organizers**
assessment of, 121
chart, 70, 83, 92–93, 94
grading of, 121
K-W-L, 27, 39, 70, 91, 92
story map, 32,
QUAD, 91,
web, 49, 65, 93
**Groups/grouping,** 9–10, 11–14, 16, 17, 22, 36, 67, 70, 79, 107–108, 111, 126
*See also* Classroom management and Heterogeneous
**Group retelling, 83**

**Hammond, W. Dorsey,** 15, 27, 44, 69, 109
**Handwriting,** 86
**Hemisphericity Theory,** 56
**Heterogeneous grouping,** 13–14
**Home language maintenance,** 80–81
**Hopkins, Lee Bennett,** 101

**Individual needs**
*See* Meeting individual needs
**Informal assessment,** 10, 43, 49–50, 121–122, 125–127, 137–139

**Informal language,** 72–73
**Integrated curriculum**
language arts, 29–30, 70, 125
reading strategies, 31
spelling, 115–117
vocabulary, 109–111
writing
*See* Writing
**Integrated instruction,** 29–32, 34–36, 37–39, 40–41, 84–85, 90–91, 94–95, 96–97, 98, 103–105, 106, 109, 112–114
**Internet (use of),** 35–36
**Inquiry learning,** 10
**Invented spelling,** 88, 111, 116–117, 141, 161

**Journals,** 9, 18–20
buddy, 18,
class, 20
dialogue, 18, 20, 31
diaries, 19
daily/personal, 19, 65, 70, 89
primary children and, 20
response, 19, 21, 27, 31, 70, 89, 108

**Kid watching,** 49–50, 125, 128, 133–135, 155
**K-W-L**
*See* Graphic organizers
**Krashen, Stephen,** 74, 112
**Kutiper, Karen,** 21

**Language acquisition**
*See* Students Acquiring English
**Learning centers,** 7, 14, 36, 67, 68, 70, 151
**Learning logs,** 19
*See also* Journals
**Learning styles,** 57–60, 61–63, 68, 69, 70, 71, 92–93
**Learning disabled students**
*See* Meeting individual needs
**Limited English Proficiency**
*See* Students Acquiring English
**Listening,** 29–30, 65, 78–79, 100, 108, 113, 125, 130
**Literature**
appreciation for, 22, 99–100, 107–108
circles, 16, 22, 107–108, 150
integrating the curriculum with, 42, 43, 70, 86, 99–100, 101–102, 109
listening to, 43, 46–50, 113
logs, 18
multicultural, 106
poetry, 99–100, 101–102
response to
*See* Reader response
vocabulary and, 109, 111
writing and, 86
**Literature-based reading,** 16–17, 99–100, 101, 109, 111
**Literature mapping, 32**

**Low-achieving students,** 12, 17, 27–28, 49, 61–63, 64–65, 66–68, 80–81

**Maintaining home language,** 80–81
**Mapping,** 32, 111
**Meeting individual needs**
gifted and talented, 49, 69–71
learning styles, 57–60, 61–63, 69, 70, 71, 92–93
low-achieving students, 12, 17, 27–28, 49, 61–63, 64–65, 66–68, 80–81
multiple intelligences, 56–60, 70
reluctant readers and writers, 17, 24, 49, 66–67, 68, 85, 92–93
second-language support, 75–77, 78–79
strategies for, 16, 57–60, 61–63, 64–65, 66–67, 73, 74–77, 92–93, 100
**Metacognition,** 126
**Minilessons,** 42, 86
**Miscue analysis,** 133, 134–136
**Modalities,** 56–60
**Modeling,** 9, 10, 15, 42, 44, 46, 64–65, 66, 70, 73, 86, 89, 90–91, 111
**Multiculturalism,** 40–41, 106
**Multiple intelligences,** 56–60, 70

**Negotiated grading,** 123
**Nonfiction,** 33, 103–105
**Nonstandard English,** 72–73
**Note-taking,** 91

**Ogle, Donna,** 18, 33
**Observation**
*See* Assessment, Kid watching
**Oral language**
*See* Listening; Speaking; Choral reading; and Fluency
**Oral reading,** 32, 115–119, 128
*See also* Choral reading and Fluency

**Pacing,** 15–17
**Parent involvement**
*See* Family involvement
**Peer-Assessment,** 125, 126, 129, 152, 156, 159
**Personal response to literature**
*See* Reader response
**Phonemic awareness,** 44, 145
**Phonics**
in context, 115
as a cueing system, 115
invented spelling, 87–89, 115–117
letter names and, 44, 116–117, 145
phonemic awareness, and rules in, 28, 145, 147

spelling, and 87–89, 115–119
word families, 117
**Poetry, 83, 98, 99–100, 101–103, 110, 116**
**Portfolios, 10, 24, 123, 148, 149–154**
*See also* Assessment
**Prediction, 27, 48, 65, 67, 70**
**Prewriting, 83, 86, 90–91, 94**
activities, 92–93
**Prior knowledge, 27**
**Print, conventions of, 48, 87–89, 140–141, 143**
**Print-rich environment, 89, 111**
**Process writing, 82–83, 86, 90–91, 92–93, 94–95, 96–97, 98**
**Professional resources, 166–169**
**Proofreading, 118**
**Publishing, 98**

**QUAD, 91**
**Questions, 21–22**

**Rasinski, Timothy, 160**
**Reader response, 9, 21–22, 148**
journals, 20, 89
oral language, 17, 21, 30
personal response, 21, 30, 66
response groups, 16, 17, 22, 31, 82–83, 70, 108
written
*See* Writing
**Readers' Theater, 51–56, 68, 98**
**Reading**
aloud, 17, 21, 27, 32, 65, 68
fluency, 28, 32, 51, 68
functional/real-life, 33, 37
guided, 21
independent, 15, 17, 21, 28, 68, 74–76, 112–114, 122, 151
portfolios, 148, 154, 156
response to, 148, 159
sight vocabulary, 116
spelling, and 88–89, 110, 115–117
**Reading strategies, 27–28, 32, 33, 44–45, 46, 65, 66–67, 139**
*See also* Strategic reading
**Reading styles, 61–63, 68, 71**
**Real-life skills, 33**
**Recorded books, 61–63**
**Resources**
booklists, 100, 102
glossary of professional terms, 171–173
professional bookshelf, 166–169
**Responding and revising, 83, 96–97, 154**
**Response groups**
*See* Reader response
**Response journals**
*See* journals
**Retelling, 30, 64, 65, 83, 142, 163**
**Revising**
*See* writing
**Rhyming, 99–100**
**Risk-taking, 65, 67, 71**
**Role-play, 93**

**Roser, Nancy L., 51**
**Running records, 133–135, 137–138**

**Schlagal, Robert, 118**
**Second-language learners, 72–73**
*See* Students Acquiring English
**Self-assessment (student), 10, 23–24, 25, 122, 123, 126, 128, 143, 150, 155, 156–158**
**Self-assessment (teacher), 17**
**Seminoff, Nancy, E., 34**
**Shanahan, Timothy, 94**
**Shared reading, 8, 31, 46, 47, 48, 49, 50, 68, 99, 100**
**Shared writing, 82–83**
**Skills, 16–17, 30–31, 42, 64, 68, 128, 129**
**Songs, 110**
**Sound-letter relationships**
*See* Phonics
**Smith, Patricia, 7, 37, 87**
**Speaking, 17, 29–30, 66, 78–79, 125, 130**
**Special needs, students with**
*See* Meeting Individual Needs
**Spelling, 88–89, 115–117, 118–120, 141**
**Standard English, 72–73**
**Steps to spell a word, 83, 89**
**Story elements**
*See* Literary elements
**Story map, 60, 108**
**Story, sense of, 132, 140, 141, 144**
**Storytelling, 81, 108**
**Strategic reading, 9, 46, 47, 66**
**Strategies, 25, 26, 27, 30–32, 90–91, 94–95, 96–97, 98, 125–126, 154**
**Strickland, Dorothy, 29, 42, 46, 82**
**Students Acquiring English (SAE), 72–73, 74–77, 78–79, 80–81, 114**
**Summarizing, 121, 139**

**Variant dialects, 72–73**
**Vocabulary, 68, 74–77, 80–81**
development, 109–111, 112–114
games and activities, 99, 109–110, 118–120
instructional support for, 109–110, 111
maps, 110–111
strategies, 109–110
word recognition, 27, 18–120, 115–117
word web, 49
**Voluntary reading, 21, 28, 30–32, 68, 112–114**

**Wallis, Judy, 107, 121**
**Webs**
*See* Graphic organizers
**Wepner, Shelley, B., 34**
**Word recognition**
*See* Vocabulary
**Word study, 44, 65, 118–120**
**Writing, 18–19, 29–30, 60**
activities, 29, 83, 91, 92–93, 163
assessing, 84, 87, 88, 132, 140–143, 154, 158
*See also* Assessment
assigning topics, 84, 92–93
big books, 70, 83
captions, 83
drafting, 83, 94–95
elements of effective, 84
expository, 57–58, 70, 83, 89, 92–93, 100
informal, 22, 82–85
invented spelling, 88, 116–117, 141, 160
journals
*See* Journals
literary elements in children's, 140, 141
poetry, 60, 70, 83, 100
prewriting, 83, 86, 90–92, 93–94
process, 85, 86, 90–93, 94–95, 96–97, 98
publishing, 98
records
*See* Portfolios
responding and revising, 83, 96–97, 154
self-selected topics, 84
shared writing, 82–83
spelling and, 88–89, 111, 141–143, 158
stages in emergent, 87–89, 115–117, 140–143, 158
stories, 68, 92–93, 132, 140
word choice in, 88, 140
**Writing centers, 89**
**Writing workshops, 9, 84–85, 87, 88, 89, 150**

**Yukota, Junko, 106**

**Teacher empowerment, 16–17**
**Teacher modeling, 10, 16, 32, 64–65, 66–67, 85, 91, 118**
**Teacher resources**
*See* Resources
**Technology integration, 34–36, 97**
**Television and Children, 164–165**
**Testing**
*See* Assessment
**Themes, 37–39**
**Think-Alongs, 27, 137–139**
**Thinking**
creative, 70
critical, 164–165
hemisphericity theory, 56
learning styles, 70, 72, 78
process, 126
theories of intelligence, 56–60
**Thonis, Eleanor W., 72, 78**
**Time on task, 67**
**Tracking print, 44, 115**
**Trade books, 42, 43**
**Transitional spelling, 88, 115, 117**

© Harcourt